American Religious Leaders

DR. MUHLENBERG

BY

WILLIAM WILBERFORCE NEWTON, D. D.

BOSTON AND NEW YORK
HOUGHTON, MIFFLIN AND COMPANY
The Riverside Press, Cambridge
1890

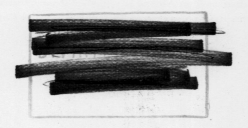

The Riverside Press, Cambridge, Mass., U. S. A.
Electrotyped and Printed by H. O. Houghton & Company.

To

THE RT. REV. HENRY C. POTTER, D. D., LL. D.

WHO, IN HAVING BEFORE HIM THE LARGE-HEARTED STANDARDS OF HIS VENERATED

FATHER, RECOGNIZES THE FACT THAT IN THE PRESENT CONSTRUCTIVE

AGE THE LOYAL CHURCHMAN IS BESET WITH PROBLEMS

WHICH, IN THEIR COMPLEXITY, THE FATHERS OF

YESTERDAY NEVER KNEW,

This Volume

IS DEDICATED WITH THE AFFECTION OF A FRIENDSHIP WHICH HAS DEEPENED

WITH TIME — THE SOLE TEST OF LIFE AS IT IS OF TRUTH — IN THE

HOPE THAT HE MAY LIVE TO SEE THE DREAM OF THE

SAINTLY MUHLENBERG REALIZED, IN THE TRUE

"EMANCIPATION OF THE EPISCOPATE,"

AND IN THE VERITABLE "UN-

SECTARIZING OF THE

CHURCH."

PREFACE.

THE life of the Rev. William Augustus Muhlenberg is the record of one of the marked leaders of American religious thought.

He had not the brilliancy of Channing, nor the logical force of Jonathan Edwards, but his character blended most harmoniously with his career, and he possessed the three great gifts of leadership, — "the sense of vision," "the discerning of spirits," and "the ability to make a movement march."

He passed in his time for a prophet and a dreamer, but to-day it is unmistakably discerned that his career furnished the formative influence of the past generation, whose manifested results we discover in the present condition of church life.

Dr. Muhlenberg touched liberalism with one hand, and institutionalism with the other hand. He founded the first church hospital. He established the free-church system by the experiment in the Church of the Holy Communion in New York city. He developed the first order of Protestant Deaconesses. He anticipated the problems of socialism in his efforts to establish St. Johnland; and he lives again in the present age, since his dream of an inter-ecclesiastical congress has become a realized fact, whose knockings at the door of the House of Bishops in Chicago have given to American Christendom the Bishops' Manifesto upon Christian Unity.

The results of this versatile and comprehensive character are making themselves felt in the church life of the present day in a most marked degree. "Your Father Abraham," said our Lord, "rejoiced to see my day, and he saw it and was glad." The man who makes an epoch may not live to see the day of its fruition, but others see it and take courage. The day of Dr. Muhlenberg has come to that church whose loyal son he delighted to be called. Parties and schools of thought have led the way up to the present epoch, but the church is larger and wider than any parties in it, and this was the one doctrine this man persistently preached. The men of his day said that he was a dreamer, that he was illogical; and so this prophet lived and died among us, and we knew not what his words meant which he spoke unto us. He stood for an evangelical pulpit, and the divine commission to preach Christ as the Saviour for men; while at the same time the Lutheranism in his nature accepted the sacramental symbolism of Germany, so that he always came to God in public worship in the form of the altar service, which typical human act Bushnell has so profoundly elaborated in his greatest theological work. He stood for a wide-heartedness which was larger than the shibboleths and formulas of any school or party, and he developed the institutionalism of the church as the only basis upon which any true growth and enlargement could take place. He called himself an "Evangelical Catholic," and at last his day of influence and power, which has been long in coming, has dawned. This volume contains the story of Dr. Muhlenberg's life and the salient features of his ministry, the one aim in view having been to sketch the life, and let this tell the story of the character of him who lived it. To rightly describe the life

of such a worker as this is in itself a task worthy
of one possessing more time than it is mine to
give; but I have thought twice before declining
to do this work, having realized that, by portray-
ing this character for the generation to come, it
might be that a lasting impulse would make
itself felt through the veins of the church of the
future, if this strong life could stand for the
coming years as the symbol of a bold, aggressive
Christianity, without fear and without apology,
— a Christianity whose face is set towards solv-
ing the hard problems of the future with a resolute courage and a determined will.

There is quoted at length in this book Dr.
Muhlenberg's wonderful prevision of the second
step towards Christian unity as contained in the
Memorial Movement, namely, the question of
ordination. The church has waited thirty years
before it has taken the first step towards unity
as pictured in his inter-ecclesiastical congress.
There is also sketched as simply as possible Dr.
Muhlenberg's practical solution of this next step,
the hard problem of ordination and organic oneness, in the hope that this might prove the direct
message of the hour for which the church has

been waiting, and that once again the minds of to-day might trouble this sleeping Samuel so that he might appear again and speak to the church, that it inquire honestly of the Lord and then go boldly forward. It would be vain and unmeaning work, after the valuable and complete life of Dr. Muhlenberg written by Miss Anne Ayers, as well as the indirect references to his ministry in the full and copious letters produced by the Rev. Hall Harrison in his life of Bishop Kerfoot, to write another detailed biography of this eminent father of yesterday in the Episcopal Church in America. But it never can be other than helpful to study out such a character, and build into structural unity the gathered words and works of a great creative mind, whose influence lives on as a motive power long after the grave has closed over that which is mortal. Such is the object of this study of the life and character of this remarkable man.

This book has made been possible through the coöperation of my friend the Rev. Preston Barr, whose judgment, aid, and most helpful criticism have been invaluable factors in its creation.

It is called a study rather than a life, for it

has been the purpose of the writer to bring out the relationship of Dr. Muhlenberg's personality and work to the subsequent development of Christianity in America resulting from his life, rather than to describe again those facts in his life which have been already given to the public in his published memoir. What has been here attempted has been the perspective view of his life and influence, the background and the fore-ground of the picture, with this striking person-ality standing as the central figure of the church's present-day liberalized life.

There have been many bishops and doctors who have been leaders in the church as preach-ers, workers, thinkers, and writers, but the mag-netic finger of the present age points unerringly to Muhlenberg as after all the truest representa-tive of that national and historic church which professes to be both Catholic and Protestant, the strange paradox of which is solved by the simple and beautiful life of this unconscious " leader of religious thought."

WM. WILBERFORCE NEWTON.

ST. STEPHEN'S RECTORY, PITTSFIELD,
    January 1, 1890.

CONTENTS.

———•———

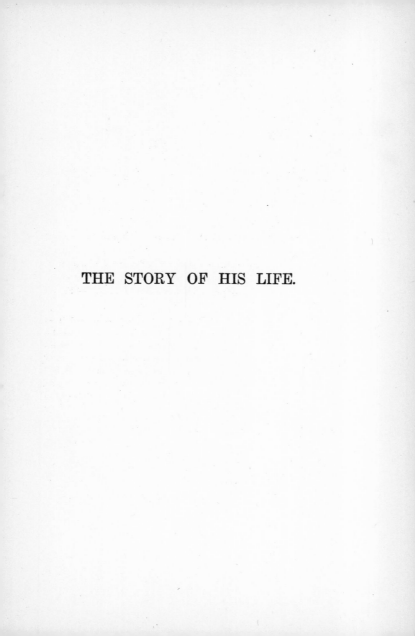

THE STORY OF HIS LIFE.

"There was a care on my mind so to pass my time that nothing might hinder me from the most steady attention to the voice of the true Shepherd." — JOHN WOOLMAN.

"Life has two ecstatic moments, — one when the spirit catches sight of truth, the other when it recognizes a kindred spirit. Perhaps it is only in the land of truth that spirits can discern each other, as it is when they are helping each other on that they may best hope to arrive there." — HARE, *Guesses at Truth*.

"It is better to be useful than brilliant. You do not think so? Well, then, your heart does not beat to the same music which regulated the pulse of the Apostle Paul." — F. W. ROBERTSON.

"Some people find religion a burden; others regard it as an indifferently useless religious institution in which they desire no share, and concerning which they never trouble themselves again. Others, again, look upon it as the mainstay of their lives, and there are those whose interests in this world are not strong enough to shake their faith in the next, whose passions do not get the mastery, and whose self is sheltered from danger by something more than the feeble defense of an accomplished egotism." — F. MARION CRAWFORD, *Saracinesca*.

WILLIAM AUGUSTUS MUHLENBERG.

CHAPTER I.

THE STORY OF HIS LIFE.

I.

1796–1815.

IN the summer of 1795, when the new-born nation of the United States was agitated to a point of childish frenzy over the Jay Treaty, and when it was extremely doubtful if the bills necessary for the enforcement of its terms would pass the House of Representatives, a merchant of Philadelphia is reported to have said to a prominent member of that body: "If you do not give us [the Federalists] your vote, your Henry shall not have my Polly." The speaker in this interview was Mr. William Sheafe, a gentleman of German origin, and "Polly" was his daughter Mary, whose hand had been asked in marriage by Henry William Muhlenberg, eldest son of Frederick A. Muhlenberg, speaker

of the House of Representatives of the First
Congress, and again of the Second, during
Washington's first administration. It was discovered that the vote so urgently demanded in
the interests of peace by this representative of
the mercantile class was already determined as
desired ; Polly was accordingly given to Henry,
and on the 16th of September, 1796, became
the mother of William Augustus Muhlenberg.[1]

[1] Frederick A. Muhlenberg was not reëlected to the speaker-
ship in 1795, but as chairman of the Committee of the Whole
House he gave the casting vote which saved the treaty, and
probably the country from revolution. In McMaster's *History
of the People of the United States*, the excitement connected
with the adoption of the celebrated Jay Treaty is thus graph-
ically described : —

"When it was known that Washington had at last put his
name to the instrument (the Jay Treaty), the Republican
journals broke out in abuse. 'The President,' said the *Aurora*,
'has violated the Constitution. He has made a treaty with a
nation that is the abhorrence of our people. He has treated
our remonstrances with pointed contempt. Louis XVI., in the
meridian of his splendor and his power, never dared to heap
such insults upon his subjects. The answer to the respectful
remonstrances of Boston, Philadelphia, and New York sounds
like the words of an omnipotent director of a seraglio. He has
thundered contempt upon the people with as much confidence
as if he sat upon the throne of Indostan. As he has been dis-
respectful to his people, let him no longer expect them to view
him as a saint.' " — Vol. ii. p. 249.

For Washington's letter to John Jay, see Sparks's *Writings
of George Washington*, vol. x. p. 404.

See, also, *Memoirs of the Administrations of Washington and
Adams, edited from the Papers of Roger Wolcott*, by George
Gibbs, vol. ii. 319.

Through the paternal line this child had a clear title to a patrimony of both character and mental power; for the Muhlenberg family was one of the most conspicuous and honorable in the period of our later colonial, and early national history. Its founder in this country was "the blessed and venerable Henry Melchior Muhlenberg,"[1] or "Father Muhlenberg," as he was popularly called. Born at Hanover in the year 1711, he had been educated under the great Francke at Halle. His apostolic zeal led him through a missionary career of heroic devotion and unremitting toil — in the course of which he established the Lutheran Church on the shores of the New World.

As the writer stood recently before the walls of the celebrated institution founded by Francke at Halle, and witnessed the extended range of its marvelous benefactions, he could not but be impressed with the fact of the far-reaching effect of the inspiration of human character as shown in the personality of Francke, who, in the heart of Saxony, — the land of the liberating Luther, — with a divine and helpful power, had educated a Muhlenberg in one generation, and had inspired in another century his greater descendant with the vision of St. Johnland, taken in part from "The Franckeschen Stiftungen" in a German university town.

[1] Quoted from his epitaph.

This memorable and worthy man, Father Muhlenberg, had three sons. The eldest of these, John Peter Gabriel Muhlenberg, took orders both in the Lutheran Church and in the Church of England. After having passed from the care of a parish in Virginia to the colonelcy of a regiment in the War of the Revolution, he rose to the rank of major-general, by virtue of honorable and distinguished services. Henry Ernst, the youngest son, spent his life as a devoted pastor of the Lutheran communion, and also achieved some distinction as an author and original investigator in the science of botany; while Frederick Augustus, the second son, and the grandfather of the subject of this volume, has been already referred to as a statesman of eminence at the period of the formation of our national government. At the age of nine years the shadow of grief fell across the pathway of the little William Augustus in the sudden death of his father from apoplexy, after which bereavement his mother with her three children — himself, a younger brother and sister — went to live with his grandmother, Mrs. Sheafe, in Philadelphia. With this period began his education at the Philadelphia Academy under the tuition of the Rev. Dr. Abercrombie, an Episcopal clergyman of considerable prominence. His mother was of the Lutheran faith; but as the children

were ignorant of the German language, in which
the Lutheran services were then conducted,
they were left to their own choice of a church
for Sunday worship, and that of William and
his sister fell upon Christ Church, of which
Bishop White was rector. The boy soon developed a strong and loyal liking for the church,
whose worship seemed instantly to quicken the
latent veneration and enthusiasm of his rich,
warm nature into active and conscious exercise.

A sort of dramatic instinct for the realization
of sacred offices was one of the marked manifes-
tations of his childish years. One is reminded
by this child-life of the boyhood of Thomas Chal-
mers, when we read that in his eighth year the
little William, already possessed by the purpose
of becoming a clergyman, was accustomed to
hold church service on Sunday evenings, with
the family for auditors, going through the form
of preaching, not in play, but with sober sincer-
ity, choosing a text, and treating it with as much
earnestness and thought as he could bring to the
task ; or of the childhood of John Henry Newman, when we learn of his quick appreciation of
sacred symbolism, of his love for the solemnities
and joys of festival and fast, and of his unvarying delight in the mystic significance of the
Christian Year. All the extant evidences agree

in representing him as a child of tender and vivid sensibility; of quick and keen intelligence; a merry, genial playfellow, overflowing with droll and sparkling humor; fastidious, energetic, ingenious ; with an eager eye for beauty, a sensitive ear for harmony; with tastes that gave emphatic promise of that ecclesiastical æstheticism so little understood or appreciated in his after-years; and withal a joyous, deep, affectionate, intuitive religiousness that made itself apparent in the earliest operations of intelligence. Of his academic career there is nothing recorded that is especially striking in character.

He graduated from the Philadelphia Academy in his twelfth year, and spent the three following years in the grammar school of the University of Pennsylvania, preparatory to entering upon his collegiate training in that institution. During the following period, from his fifteenth to his nineteenth year, he gave decided indications of that sturdy independence and originality which marked his after-life. A distinct and undisguised dissatisfaction under the restraints and limitations of the curriculum possessed him during these college years. This is susceptible of easy explanation, in view of the fact that the average college course of eighty years ago would hardly compare favorably with that of the preparatory school of to-day. Not only were there no elective studies, in which the student of to-day has opportunity to follow his inclinations in some practical direction, or to rise on the wings of his aspiration in expansive and congenial elements of knowledge, but a mechanical monotony of method and of drill, which could not but prove wearisome and vexatious to a free and aspiring nature, formed the entire university life.

One is not surprised, therefore, to learn that Muhlenberg expanded the range of his intellectual vision beyond the narrow limits of the curriculum into the regions of music, drawing, elocution, chemistry, botany, and mineralogy. His natural taste and talent for music determined him to the choice of the former of these studies, while his desire for a wider culture and a more practical training led him to engage in the latter. For mathematics he had neither aptitude nor liking, pursuing this study only as a necessary part of his collegiate work. The moral fibre of his nature showed its quality, at the expense of much temporary unpopularity, in his indignant denunciation of the tricks of his classmates upon the venerable provost of the university, whom they had chosen without any reason as the favorite victim of their boyish pranks and unmanly behavior.

During these years his religious instincts developed rapidly, and on Easter Day, 1813, he received the apostolic rite of Confirmation, with one hundred and eighty others, at the hands of Bishop White. Of all the subjects that fill the pages of his boyish journal, none is entered with such minuteness of detail and with such manifest enthusiasm and delight, as that of his religious thoughts and occupations. His experiences, of which his diary has preserved a faithful and extended transcript, were preëminently of the joyous, natural, spontaneous order. Nothing is morbid, subjective, or factitious.

The record of religious conversations, of services and sermons on Sundays and holy days, of his spiritual efforts in behalf of his college companions and friends, constitutes what we know of his religious life at that time. Of gloomy introspection and despair, of feverish ecstasy and unnatural transports, no trace can be found. In harmony with his religious character was his conscientious aversion to war, which amounted to a Quaker-like antipathy to everything military. All the excitement and dangers of the war of 1812–14 awakened in him no thrill of military enthusiasm. On the contrary, the stirring news of the death of General Ross, after the capture of Washington, only elicited the query in his diary, " Is it Christian-like to

rejoice in the death of an enemy?" with the remark, "New Testament says, 'Love your enemies.'" The character of Napoleon he intensely
and energetically detested.

In reviewing the dawning youth of this remarkable man, which closed at his graduation
with honor in January, 1815, the strong and
effective traits which distinguished his manhood
are already conspicuously evident. His devout
and manly religiousness; his quick perception
of the defects and limitations of the existing
order in social and ecclesiastical life; his strong
practical sense and organizing genius; his deep
and tender personal sympathy; the strength
and fidelity of his youthful attachments; the
intensity of his personal solicitude for the welfare of others; his native tact and instinctive
discernment of the principles of leadership, —
all these delicate, complex, and intimately related elements of character were actively ger-
minant during his collegiate years.

II.

1817–1825.

On September 18, 1817, having two days before attained the age of twenty-one years, William
Augustus Muhlenberg was ordered deacon by

Bishop White, and soon after was made assistant or chaplain to the bishop in the rectorship of Christ Church, St. Peter's, and St. James', Philadelphia, for which position, at the urgent invitation of the bishop, he had given up, before receiving orders, a projected visit to Europe.

These were days when theological seminaries were unknown, and so it came to pass that the young candidate read Paley, Butler, Stackhouse, and Adam Clarke with a clerical preceptor, the Rev. Jackson Kemper, afterwards the pioneer bishop of the Northwest, and at that time one of the assistant ministers of the united churches under Bishop White's pastoral care. From this teacher he at the same time received much benefit in the way of active initiation into the practical work of a parish. During the three years of his diaconate he was occupied with the usual duties of a parish assistant, preaching in his turn only with the bishop and the other assistants, and devoting his main energies to Sunday - school work and the visitation of the poor. In October, 1820, he was advanced to the priesthood by Bishop White, and shortly afterwards accepted a call to the rectorship of St. James' Church, Lancaster, to the great disappointment of the Bishop, who had hoped to retain his services as chaplain and assistant.

It is impossible without emotion to survey the

opening hours of any earnest and fruitful human ministry; and there is enough in the personality and possibilities of young Muhlenberg to kindle the flame of a hopeful imagination at the contemplation of his dawning career. But to the new-made priest himself, there was doubtless little in his outlook that seemed specially calculated either to excite the sensibilities or inspire the imagination.

The Lancaster to which he was called was a crude section of the peasant and middle class Germany of the eighteenth century, transplanted to the soil of the New World, where, by the end of the first quarter of the nineteenth century, it presented a curious specimen of arrested development. A more unromantic environment than that of this unaspiring and sordid community never vexed the soul of a poet, as the young clergyman soon proved himself to be. A Low-German society without ideas, without refinement, almost without language, — its vocabulary to this day numbers not a thousand words, — stolid, immobile, unresponsive, — such were the depressing elements that characterized this region. Its ideal of an Eden was a Dutch farm, with a Dutch village in the background, such as Washington Irving has described with such subtle humor in the vivid sketches of his "Knickerbocker's History of New York." Everything

moved on the earthly plane, and the air was
heavy with the vapors of a dead and decompos-
ing materialism. Into this uncongenial, unim-
pressible, and unappreciative element of stupid
and obstinate conservatism came the young
prophet from the East, like the lady in Milton's
" Mask of Comus," with his great warm heart,
his practical notions of progress, his striking
presence, and his undoubted gift of leadership.

In personal appearance Muhlenberg was tall
and well-proportioned. His head was of mas-
sive structure, well set, and crowned with an
abundance of curling locks. Both in face and
bearing he was marvelously impressive. His
portrait presents a remarkable combination of
masculine strength of feature with feminine gentleness of expression. The brow is broad and
full, the nose is imperial, the mouth is large, the
lower lines of the face are regular and powerful.
There is an expression of indescribable benig-
nity, not unmingled with humor, in the eye ; and
the softened downward lines give an effect of
almost motherly tenderness and affection. When
animated or interested in any of his benevolent
designs, there was a peculiar radiancy in his
countenance and manner, that indicated the essential purity of the spirit within. With his
rare gifts and great power of personal attraction, he might readily have become, if he had

chosen, a Chrysostom in the pulpit. But he perceived that he lived in a different age from that
of the Greek theologian, — an age which was to
be influenced in quite other ways, and which demanded of him something better than the glit-
tering and far-sounding reputation of a popular preacher. The children of the community
around him were growing up in an ignorance as
dense and prejudiced as that which gave their
parents such self-complacent satisfaction. His
first move, therefore, after organizing a Sunday-
school and other educational interests in his
own parish, was one in behalf of public education ; and in this movement he displayed in a
signal manner two great qualities which characterized him throughout his entire life, — the faculty for leadership, and the genius for organization. Instead of inviting the certain opposition
and contempt of the community by taking them
into his counsels, he quietly instigated and carried through the legislature of the State, a bill
making the city of Lancaster the second public
school district in the State, Philadelphia being
the first. The matter attracted no attention until a large building designed for a school-house
was begun, at an estimated cost of $10,000, to
be defrayed from public funds already appro-
priated for the purpose. Then at last the German citizens were indignant, and hastened to

remonstrate against the injustice of legislating
for schools to be taught in the English language
only; but their harmless ill-humor, of the
Wouter Van Twiller type, which was too inert
to accomplish anything more than bluster, had
ample time to work itself off after the building
was completed, and during the period in which
Mr. Muhlenberg was organizing the new public
school system of the place.   In this he was inde-
fatigable, and in a high degree successful; and
from this experience in Lancaster, at the opening of his ministry, dates the dawn of his aspirations and purposes in the direction of that
educational work in which he was to impart a
new conception to the public of his time, and to
which a great part of his most faithful energies
were to be devoted.   It was here, too, that he first
evinced in a practical way that powerful influence over the young of his own sex which ever
afterwards distinguished him.   In the school
was a bright little boy of six or seven years, in
whom Mr. Muhlenberg saw, with his unerring
insight, the elements of future force of character.   One's memory delights to linger over the
scene in which Mr. Muhlenberg placed this little fellow — at the age of nine — " on a large
table under a sort of canopy of oak leaves and
boughs, and stood beside him to encourage him,"
while, " in the presence of a large company, the

juvenile orator pronounced to General Lafayette, on his visit to the school in 1825, his own pre-composed address of welcome."

Under such circumstances began his life-long interest and friendship for the future educator and bishop, John B. Kerfoot.

It was also during the Lancaster period in his life that he achieved his first reputation as a writer of hymns. The hymn, " I would not live alway," was written in the year 1824, and immediately upon its publication sprang into an amazing popularity. The verdict of the future, however, in reference to this hymn, will in all probability be that of its author's riper years. Judged even by present standards, it belongs to an inferior order of hymnody, and Mr. Muhlenberg was as much surprised as any of his circle of friends at the wonderful favor bestowed upon it by the public. In after-years, when its widespread and continued popularity, together with his own more just and real knowledge of life, gave him a closer conviction of its faults, he strove by repeated revisions and successive versions to give it a higher and more healthful tone, — one which was more in accord with genuine Christian faith and cheer. Its intense subjectivity, its morbid depreciation of the joys of earthly existence, and its failure to recognize any significance in the discipline of life, — faults

feebly atoned for by the impatient desire of
heavenly felicity, — were elements which jarred
on the sensitive fibre of his maturer piety. One
at least of the subsequent versions for its improvement, which his dissatisfaction with the
poem led him to attempt, the version of 1876,[1]
is incomparably superior to the form in which
this hymn is popularly known. It is a sugges-
tive commentary on the contemporary taste in
matters of hymnology that his little hymn beginning, "Since o'er thy footstool," — a lyric
worthy of comparison with some of the most re-
nowned productions in this field, and written in
the same year as his famous hymn, — was allowed to go unrecognized, and is even yet almost
unknown. This first effusion was a true expression of contemporary evangelical thought: it ac-
curately embodied the average sentiment of the
day as to the dark and sad unmeaningness of life;
it expressed the curiosity of current piety to ex-
change the gloom of this discordant world for
the definite delights of the world to come, and
this doubtless accounts for much of its popularity. There was in it nevertheless a genuine
spark of the divine fire, sufficient to indicate its
author's title to the possession of poetic gifts of
no mean order.

With his poetical facility and insight were

[1] See Appendix, A.

combined a refined and exquisite musical taste
and a high degree of proficiency in the musical
art, which he exercised at intervals in his laborious life, by way of refreshment and diversion, in
the composition of sacred airs and chants. This
delicate and sensitive side of his nature found little satisfaction in the poverty of the church worship of his day with reference to the element of
hymnody ; and prompted by his own keen sense
of the need, he was himself the first to initiate
any decided and successful movement for its improvement in this particular. There were but
fifty-six hymns embodied in the prayer-book collection of the time, the bulk of which consisted
of mechanical and awkward versions of the
Psalms for metrical singing. In the year 1821
appeared his tract entitled " A Plea for Christian Hymns," in the form of a letter to a friend
in the General Convention of that year. Fail-
ing in his attempt to accomplish any action in
that complex body, which he served as secretary
of the " House of Bishops," he prepared a selection of metrical psalms and hymns from different sources. This book he named " Church
Poetry," which he introduced forthwith in the
worship of his own parish. His action in this
respect furnished a precedent which was readily
followed by a number of like-minded friends
throughout the country. As the result of this

firm and positive course, the next General Convention, fearing lest clerical liberty might assert itself in some unchurchly manner, appointed a committee on the subject of psalms and hymns, of which committee Mr. Muhlenberg was a member. The outcome of their labors was a new and enlarged collection, adopted by both houses in the year 1826, embracing several of Mr. Muhlenberg's own composition, among which we find the familiar hymns " Shout the glad tidings," " Saviour, who thy flock art feeding," " Like Noah's weary dove," " How short the race our friend has run," and " I would not live alway." [1] The melancholy strain of this famous hymn was for a long time commonly attributed to the unhappy termination of a tender passage in his experience at Lancaster. While conceding that he had formed an attachment in those years which had come to a sad and disappointing end, we are assured that the affair had not reached its depressing and unfortunate phase when the hymn in question was written; we have his own words in a published interview, also, to the same effect.

[1] This last, at first rejected, was afterwards restored at the urgent request of Dr. Onderdonk.

III.

1826–1844.

In the summer of 1826, Dr. Muhlenberg attained the age of thirty years. During the five and a half years of his pastorate he had gained a practical insight into the great wants of the world, and had also come into a distinct consciousness of his own mission in relation to them. In the midst of those years of pressing and arduous labor, so fruitful in permanent results of good, he had passed the wilderness period of his life, and had emerged into the clear and bracing atmosphere of a definite, distinct, and individual vocation. Out of the vexatious oppositions and misconceptions against which he had battled with unvarying success in his hitherto unpromising field, there had come to him the sacred vision of a new and holy calling which demanded the devotion of his life and of all its energies. He had counted the cost, and his mind had come to a firm and definite resolution. On the one hand he saw an assured future of pulpit eminence and ecclesiastical influence, towards which he was urged by the counsel of his dearest friends and by the consciousness of his own powers; on the other lay an untried experiment, involving many years of obscure and unremunerative drudgery, with the possibility of ultimate failure, so far as his own exertions went, as his personal reward. Like the awakened Saul of Tarsus, here was one who was not disobedient to the heavenly vision which was even then dawning upon his mind. And thus it came to pass that the gifted young preacher and faithful pastor, with his fine equipments and faculties, turned away from the brilliant prospects opening before him to become " a schoolmaster," "a mere teacher of boys." Some of his brethren in the ministry openly smiled over his projected plan, while others were indifferent or sought to dissuade him from the enterprise.   But his face was set towards this Jerusalem which was before him, and it was useless to try to turn him from his chosen life's work by friendly and superficial entreaties. The project was not born of a desire for praise, or for mere notoriety. Without a word of encouragement or sympathy from those of his own household, whether of the flesh or of the faith, he was minded to become an educator for the sake of the kingdom of God upon earth.   And thus it is that he stands first in the honored line of those who have considered it a sacred privilege, and one honestly included within the functions of their holy office, to teach unruly boys how to become strong and holy men.   What his ideas respecting education, what the public exigencies which determined him to the choice of this new field of labor, and what his qualifications for it were, will be set forth at length in a future chapter of this book. For the present it is enough to know that, without any thought as to when or where his vision was to be realized, he resigned his pastorate at Lancaster in the summer of 1826, and like Abraham of old, in obedience to the call of God, he went forth not knowing whither he went. His first thought was of a voyage to Europe for the study of foreign institutions and methods as a better qualification for his enterprise.

This subordinate plan came to naught, however, at the moment when he had brought it to maturity, while at the same time his ultimate purpose was thereby unexpectedly realized. During a brief visit to his family in New York, previous to embarking upon the contemplated voyage, he was casually invited to officiate one day at the Sunday services in St. George's Church, Flushing, L. I. His services were immediately followed by an invitation to the rectorship of the parish, then vacant. He compromised with the vestry by taking charge of the parish for six months, with the pleasurable anticipation of spending the interval before his voyage in intercourse with his family, after his six years of separation from them. In the very beginning of this interval, however, he was accidentally brought into communication with some gentlemen who were contemplating the erection of an academy building in Flushing.

After very little negotiation he was induced to give up his projected visit to Europe, and enter upon the headship of the proposed academy. Plans were immediately drawn up and the work begun under the direction of an incorporated company, of whom Mr. Muhlenberg was to hire the building at a certain annual percentage on the amount of its cost.

The corner-stone of the new building was laid in August, 1827, and for ten years thereafter he devoted himself with undiminished enthusiasm and unwearying effort to the work and functions of head master and teacher within its walls. From the very first, the success of his venture was assured, the individuality and effectiveness of his methods, the wonderful attraction of his personality, and the character and influence of the school, all conspired to bring him swiftly into fame as one of the foremost, as he was the most original and successful, educator of his time.

Not unlike his illustrious European predecessor in the field of education, Pestalozzi, Mr. Muhlenberg was called upon to grapple with

the stern problem of limited means and financial
embarrassment in his new venture; but, unlike
the former, he was an able and most successful
financier in all his undertakings, and in this his
first independent enterprise he achieved a signal
triumph in spite of unforeseen and unavoidable
difficulties. At the end of the third year the
new institute had absorbed all his private means,
and burdened him beside with a debt of $10,000;
yet in due time, under his prudent and skillful
management, this debt was cleared, the institution became self-supporting, and an ever-increas-
ing number of applicants was knocking at the
doors for admission.

Encouraged by this most cheering and substantial success, Mr. Muhlenberg pushed on to the
development of a higher department of his plan,
in the foundation and thorough equipment of a
college in accordance with his idea of the higher
Christian education. Declining several flattering
invitations to the headship of important institutions, he purchased, in the summer of 1835, a
farm of 175 acres near the institute, fronting on
the East River for more than a mile. This beautiful domain, which was most admirably adapted
to its intended purpose, he named College Point,
and immediately began preparations for the
erection of suitable permanent buildings, to be
known as St. Paul's College. But in the very

hour when his prospects in this direction were
the brightest, when the corner-stone of the new
institution had been laid, and all was going
smoothly forward to a happy consummation, the
whole enterprise was brought to a violent stand-
still, and ultimately wrecked, by the sudden
financial collapse of 1837. Instead of the stately
edifice of stone which was already begun, he
was compelled to shelter the infant college in a
commodious wooden building, in the hope that,
when the storm which had brought financial
ruin to most of the wealthy benefactors, who
were pledged to assist the enterprise, had spent
itself, the work so untimely suspended would be
renewed, and his fair scheme carried to completion. In this hope he was doomed to disappointment. Notwithstanding his many endeavors and appeals, the funds for the completion of
the permanent building, which he had begun on
a generous and stately plan, could not be raised;
and its foundation stones and basement walls
long remained as a visible rebuke to the church
and Christian public for thus allowing defeat
to overtake the plans of one of the world's
most devoted benefactors. The work of the college continued, however, for eight years after
its formal opening, in the temporary buildings
which Dr. Muhlenberg had found means to
erect. The work was in the hands of a faculty

of nine professors and five instructors, several of whom had been educated in the institute at Flushing; and it is quite certain that the most efficient and durable results in Dr. Muhlenberg's educational career were achieved during the eight years of the existence of St. Paul's College. At the end of these years of patient waiting he found it impracticable to go on with the work which he had so much at heart. The inadequate buildings, the lack of endowment, the want of a corporate character and power to confer degrees,[1] — these and a score of other practical difficulties were pointing with a steady and increasing emphasis to the probable dissolution of the institution in the not distant future.

Another consideration which reconciled him to the thought of withdrawal from this chosen field of labor, was the conviction that he had accomplished his mission in this department of effort in having originated and successfully managed a learned institution of a new and genuinely Christian type.

This conviction was due to the sudden appearance and rapid growth in different parts of the country, of schools organized and conducted upon the principle of St. Paul's. No bishop considered his diocese as complete without such

[1] Owing solely to the refusal of the state legislature to grant a charter to a religious institution.

an institution; and Mr. Muhlenberg was constantly importuned by such to transfer his plant, or interviewed by them for the purpose of acquiring his methods.

The necessity of thus relinquishing the college was accentuated at the same time by a call to a widely different field of work which seemed to offer most inviting possibilities. His sister, Mrs. Mary A. Rogers, in fulfillment of the purposes of her deceased husband, contemplated the building of a free church in the city of New York, and naturally looked to her brother as a suitable pastor of the church. Such an opening was one altogether to his mind. With that practical insight which characterized him in life, he had long recognized, in the necessity for a practical reformation of the church along the lines of parochial administration and a broadened general policy, a sphere of activity not less urgent than that in which, by eighteen years of his consecrated toil and genius, a practical reform of educational methods and principles had been so auspiciously inaugurated. He had already devoted much patient thought to the practical problems of church work and organization; and now that an opportunity presented itself for the embodiment of his ideal of a parish, he closed the door decisively upon the educational passage of his life, and with his eye upon two distinct

and practical objects in the line of ecclesiastical
development, the one near and the other remote,
entered with all the enthusiasm of youthful
vigor, and all the mature wisdom of meridian
manhood, upon the most protracted, brilliant,
successful, and beneficent chapter of his prolonged and fruitful ministry.

IV.

1845–1877.

When Dr. Muhlenberg began his ministry in
New York, his personality was at the zenith of
its power. He had almost completed his fiftieth
year, and his prolific genius, trained to the highest
degree of practical efficiency by the experience of
a quarter of a century in actual service, had found
a province wide enough for its most varied and
productive exercise. The feature of his character which most impresses the general reader
at this distance of time is the strong, judicious,
practical quality of all his benevolent aims. The
unspotted saintliness of his life was modestly
withdrawn into such unobtrusive and sacred
seclusion from the world that it was known only
to the very few who enjoyed the privilege of his
intimate friendship. But the naturalness of the
man, his robust common sense, the healthful

flow of intellectual high spirits, and the tender glow of his gentleness and Christian charity, hedged him round with respect and veneration wherever he was known; while his projected schemes and labors of love, that were perpetually crystallizing themselves in institutions of permanent practical benefit to the race, have immortalized his name in a group of monuments more enduring than the studied efforts of mere material grandeur. For more than thirty years he was the most capable, energetic, and successful personality of the metropolis in humanitarian activity, as he was for a long stretch of years the most potent influence in the work of reorganizing a dismembered and paralyzed Christendom.

He began this long ministry of divine compassion in the very humble and practical task of organizing and serving that which seemed to be a country parish in the neighborhood of New York; but his prophetic eye saw in advance that this rural spot, now the corner of Sixth Avenue and Twentieth Street, which he had selected for the site of the new church, would in a very few years be the centre of that swarming metropolis. Having chosen the plan and superintended the building of the house of worship, he entered on his new pastorate in the spring of 1846, and for upwards of twelve years continued, as rector of the church, to shape and guide its development.

The name which he had given to this offspring
of his heart was "The Church of the Holy
Communion." This name was a product of his
conception of the church as a family or brotherhood, with communion or fellowship in the
spirit and love of Christ as the law and method
of its life. The following extract from his address at the laying of the corner-stone, July 24,
1844, displays the spirit and aim with which he
entered on the work : —

"Let this sanctuary be called the Church of the
Holy Communion. Nor let it be only a name. Let
it be the ruling idea in forming and maintaining the
church, and in all its ministrations. Here let there
be a sanctuary consecrated specially to fellowship
in Christ, and to the great ordinance of his love.
This will rebuke all the distinctions of pride and
wealth. . . . As Christians dare not bring such distinctions to the table of the Lord, there, at least, remembering their fellowship in Christ and their common level in redemption, the high and the low, the
rich and the poor, gathered around the sacred board ;
so let the same brotherhood prevail, let there be no
places for the differences of worldly rank in the
Church of the Holy Communion." [1]

This lofty ideal of human brotherhood and
the exalted aim of realizing it as a visible embodiment, dominated and pervaded all the work

[1] See *Evangelical Catholic Papers*, Second Series, p. 79.

of those twelve years in connection with the
Church of the Holy Communion ; and by the
impulse and inspiration of this Christly ideal
were developed his two great subsequent undertakings, — St. Luke's Hospital and the Industrial Community of St. Johnland. It was this
character of practical beneficence in all his work,
flowing out in copious and unfailing currents
from the secret springs of a holy and devoted
life of personal love to Christ, which impressed
his personality upon the spirit and institutions
of his church and time with such instant and
telling effect. It is this that has attracted the
attention of the whole Christian public to him
as the preëminent leader of religious development which the Protestant Episcopal communion
has produced in this Western world. Others
were possessed of better logical powers in the
arena of controversy, or in the formulation and
adjustment of inflexible and contradictory details in theological and ecclesiastical theory, but
to Dr. Muhlenberg alone belongs the twofold
distinction of having realized, throughout his
entire ministry of more than fifty-five years,
the practical evidences of Christianity as proclaimed by his Divine Master, — " the blind see,
the lame walk, the lepers are cleansed, the deaf
hear, and to the poor the gospel is preached;"
and also of having for more than forty of those

years labored and pleaded with heroic insistence for the literal fulfillment of the Saviour's dying prayer for his people, "That they all may be one, as thou Father art in me, and I in thee; that they all may be one in us, that the world may believe that thou hast sent me."

Whatever Dr. Muhlenberg may be said to have been, he can never be called an impracticable dreamer. He saw realities in advance, albeit realities that were yet to come. He essayed, by the things that are not, to bring to nought the things that are; and this is always the method by which the Infinite Wisdom builds his many worlds, and his spiritual kingdom in these worlds.

No sooner had a commanding reality of the future arisen before Dr. Muhlenberg's vision than he set about, in the most childlike faith and manner, to bring it to pass. And to few men has it been granted to behold the completion of so large a measure of their undertakings. Five of the great institutional movements which he originated and personally initiated — the Christian element introduced into education, the organization of Protestant sisterhoods, the reform of parish administration as exemplified in the Free Church of the Holy Communion, realized philanthropy as seen in St. Luke's Hospital, and a true Christian socialism as witnessed in the

experiment of St. Johnland — were fully ma-
tured and developed in his own lifetime. A
sixth, the largest and grandest of all, the movement toward Christian unity, begotten by his
prayers as well as by his words and labors of
love during forty years, is now in the womb of
time, and is agitating the entire body of American Protestant Christianity with the initial
birth-throes of a grander and a purer church
than earth has as yet known.

For the thirty-two years of his residence in
New York, during which his astonishing labors
brought four of his great humanitarian projects
to fruition and laid the foundations of a reor-
ganized church life, he lived in the same plain
and modest seclusion from public notoriety or
prominence which had characterized him as " a
teacher of boys." Every dollar of his private
means, which consisted of an ample fortune
aside from his income as pastor, was absorbed
by his vast benevolent schemes, or dispensed in
private charities. We are told that, in his eager-
ness to give away all that he possessed, he would
even have worn coarser garments, had his mother
and sister, who gave him money for his tailor's
bills, permitted it. As pastor of St. Luke's Hospital he declined all salary, — except during the
last ten years, when he wanted the money to give
to a home for crippled children at St. Johnland,

— and his personal expenses were defrayed
wholly by gifts bestowed by friends for the purpose. With the exception of two brief summer
trips to Europe, he took no vacation from active
duty in all these years of continuous achievement. St. Luke's Hospital, where he occupied
a plainly furnished prophet's chamber for the
last twenty years of his life, while devoting his
main energy and time to the work of its super-
intendence and the pastoral care of its inmates,
was first ready for occupancy in the autumn of
1858, having been an object of his eager anticipation and patient striving for the twelve pre-
ceding years. The record of his personal ministrations to the patients of St. Luke's, and of
his tender care and individual oversight of the
poor while pastor of the Church of the Holy
Communion; the influence of these two institutions in great public crises, — the one a fountain
of inexhaustible blessing and comfort through
the terrible cholera scourge of 1849, the other a
source of strength and a river of peace through
the days of riot and mad violence in 1863, —
as well as their wider and more permanent influence in stimulating and forming the growth
of like institutions throughout the land, are facts
which alone would fill a volume.

There was never in his life any approach to
the methods of the religious mountebank or the

ecclesiastical charlatan. He realized most thoroughly that Christianity could not possibly work by any methods of sounding brass or tinkling cymbal. He knew that Christianity is simply the method of Jesus of Nazareth, and that the spirit of Christ never works to any effect without the Divine instrumentality of personal sympathy and human compassion manifested in the individual contact of life with life, and soul with soul. So, like his Galilean Lord, he lived among the lowly, reclaimed the erring, cheered the poor and toil-worn, taught the ignorant with a divine joy and patience, watched by the sick, prayed with the dying, and comforted the forsaken. Out of these personal ministrations and sympathies came the first suggestion of St. Luke's Hospital and St. Johnland.

He could not quietly contemplate the distressing condition of those who were stricken with sickness, in the wretched homes of the poor, to whom he gave his personal ministrations in the great city. His indignation was unbounded at the cruel neglect which coolly consigned them to death in their misery without attention or sympathy. It was not in him to rest quiet in a daily familiarity with their lot without a radical and prolonged effort to remedy a state of things so utterly inhuman. Almost from the death-bed

of one of these lowly sufferers he came to the
service of the church on St. Luke's Day (October 18, 1846), and quietly announced to the congregation that one half the offerings of that
day would be laid aside as the nucleus of a fund
for the building of a church hospital for the sick
among the poor, and that the same disposition
would be made with each returning festival.
The fraction over thirty dollars realized from
this announcement possibly justified the tinge of
scorn with which he was asked the same day
when he expected to build his hospital, and to
which he replied, "Never, if I don't make a
beginning." He lived in the future, and in that
future the hospital was as solid a reality to him
as its subsequent walls and wards have been to
others.

St. Johnland, "the child of his old age," as
he delighted to call it, grew in the same practical way out of his personal observation of the
vast needs of modern society as he met them in
his visits to the poor in the great city of New
York. There was no economic theory at the bot-
tom of this noble venture, — no cheap indignation
at social injustice or industrial maladjustment.
It was the simple endeavor of a plain Christian
man to remedy in his degree a state of things
which wrung his heart, and stirred his soul with
sympathy.

Francke at Halle, John Falk at Weimar, and Pastor Harms had done this same great work in the Old World in simple faith: why should it be thought a thing incredible that the same faith in the Divine Spirit of God could produce a like result in the metropolis of the New World?

To the work of soliciting the necessary funds, or rather of making clear to the public the nature of his plan, and the actual task of founding the new community, he devoted the last ten years of his life. He never disquieted himself in vain about the means of raising the enormous sums that were requisite for the establishment and maintenance of his huge charitable enterprises. Once convinced of the necessity for the work, he never doubted that the money would surely flow in. And the sums that passed through his hands, in all his benevolent ministrations public and private, can never be approximately estimated. He seemed to have an instinctive realization that what the Christian public most wanted was a safe and wise channel for home benevolence, and he offered himself as such a medium. How nobly he fulfilled the function, institutions and lives innumerable can bear witness. It is true of him also that he, as perhaps no other man of his time, understood the method of teaching with skill and effect the wealthy and the well-to-do how to give.

There is nothing more beautiful in all Christian biography than the spectacle of this aged saint spending the evening of his life in the labor of introducing such an experiment in Christian brotherhood as that of his beloved St. Johnland. Of the joy that he extracted from this hallowed employment through these ten years no pen may write. In these serene days of descending glory, so filled with blessed toil, he had bread to eat that the world knew not of.

A touching incident is told by the wife of a fellow-clergyman concerning their visit to the cemetery at St. Johnland, in which Dr. Muhlenberg broke out into an earnest prayer that he might be spared ten years more of active labor for the Master's cause, which prayer, like that of the pious Hezekiah when the sun-dial went back fifteen degrees, was granted literally, in the fact that ten years later, to the very month, his body was carried to the spot where his prayer had been offered.

He died " in the harness," in accordance with his often expressed wish. In the spring of 1874 he underwent his first real illness, a low malarial fever, from which, after some months' suffering, he rallied, and seemed to enjoy firm health again. But his wonted strength never returned. On Washington's Birthday, 1877, which he enthusiastically observed all his life, he was stricken down with a convulsion, after having spent the morning in listening to poor people at the hospital door, and in showing visitors, of whom there was a great crowd, over the building. He suffered much pain and languor during the six weeks that followed ; but the serenity of his Christian peace was not for an hour disturbed, nor the light of his holy joy beclouded. The strain of praise and the note of gladness were oftenest on his lips. The end came on Sunday evening, April 8th. The friend who was most intimately associated with his labor in the last thirty years of his life, and whom his words and holy influence had induced to consecrate herself to the life of a Sister, was present, and clasped his hand at the moment of release. His sister, Mrs. Rogers, and a very few relatives and friends, were also at the bedside. A prayer was offered by a clergyman who had called, after which, as they all stood watching, the shadow of death fell suddenly upon the face, which told them that the weary spirit was at rest.

THE DEVELOPMENT OF THE SCHOOL IDEA IN AMERICAN CHURCH LIFE.

"With the schoolmasters, I believe, more than with the clergy, rests the shaping of that generation which will decide in a large degree what the England of the future will be, — turbulent, divided, self-indulgent, materialized, or quickened with a power of spiritual sympathy, striving towards the realization of a national ideal, touched already with that spirit of sacrifice which regards every gift of fortune and place and character as held for the common good." — CANON WESTCOTT.

"Living contact with the young is a spring of youth. As you enter into their thoughts, you receive of their freshness. The true teacher can never grow old. He always hears the children's voices, and can understand them." — CANON WESTCOTT.

"One great characteristic of holiness is never to be exacting, — never to complain. Each complaint drags us down a degree in our upward course. If you would discern in whom God's spirit dwells, watch that person, and notice whether you ever hear him murmur." — GOLD DUST.

"Remember, this frail, evil, weak humanity of ours, these hearts that yield to almost every gust of temptation, — the Son of man hoped for them." — F. W. ROBERTSON.

CHAPTER II.

In studying the life of Dr. Muhlenberg as a leader of religious thought, it must, first of all, never be forgotten that he was in no sense a leader, or even a student, of theology. The quality of his mind was as remote as possible from the speculative habit of thought, and no merely theological idea or system ever kindled a spark of enthusiasm in his nature. He accepted the main position of the Thirty-nine Articles without opposition, and recognized in them the form of sound words which passed current as the orthodoxy of the time. There is no evidence that he ever submitted his beliefs to the test of criticism, or that troublesome doubts compelled him to enter upon any lengthened process of critical inquiry. No trace of argument or apology is anywhere to be found, in his records or remains, as revealing an undertone of doubt, misgiving, or distrust.

And thus it came to pass, for the reason that

he was seeking other results than logical conclusions, that his spiritual life was not a matter of correct opinion, but of living personal relation to the Lord Jesus Christ as a personal Saviour; his absorbing aim was not the maintenance of any set views, clear or otherwise, but the promotion of godliness in the form of inward character and outward expression. In this practical sphere the insight of his genius, the range of his sympathies, and the reach of his mental activity, are most remarkable.

In this respect he realized the mission of his apostolic prototype, the divine St. John, to whom his Master committed the care of his beloved mother, — the most visionary of the disciples in this way being charged with the most practical of duties.

His originality and foresight are conspicuous, first of all, in the fact that he was the first to appreciate the necessity of Christian education within the lines of church life and thought; and it is not too much to say that a conception of education entirely fresh and new was given by him to the rapidly developing American commonwealth. " It must not be forgotten," says the able biographer of his most distinguished pupil and associate,[1] " that the very idea of a church school as held by Dr. Muhlenberg was at that

[1] *Life of Bishop Kerfoot*, vol. i. p. 33.

time an entire novelty in our land." And another, one of a most distinguished family of educators, who belongs to the second generation in direct spiritual descent from Dr. Muhlenberg,[1] declares that " the notion of education as complex and many-sided, as an art requiring not merely the power to teach the use of certain languages or sciences, but also demanding skill, tact, knowledge of the world, generous sympathy with human infirmities, ability and quickness in comprehending the special needs of individuals, genuine literary instincts and enthusiasms, and a high moral and intellectual standard, has only begun lately to be fairly comprehended in this country. The people of the United States owe to Dr. Muhlenberg and Bishop Kerfoot a larger debt than will probably ever be acknowledged for having given to this complex idea of education impetus, development, and extension. . . . They were pioneers working in a new country, with scanty material and resources, scarcely conscious of the real largeness of their undertaking, and feeling their way to wider and more comprehensive plans and ideas under the severe training of disappointment, depreciation, and meagre support. They did not come into any broad and direct contact with their day and generation ; it

[1] The Rev. J. H. Coit, *Life of Bishop Kerfoot*, by Rev. Dr. Hall Kerfoot, p. 324.

was impossible that they should.   But their experiments, their failures, their ideas, their noble and generous ideals, — alas ! never fully realized, — have been seeds which have sprung up and borne good fruit.   Others have entered upon their labors, and the result has been the formation and diffusion of notions and standards of education which are having most beneficial influences throughout the land."

Dr. Muhlenberg's enthusiasm in education was no superficial and visionary idolatry of a method, but an intelligent devotion to an intelligent ideal, and an ideal of the most noble and practical kind.   In his view, the end of all education is the production of the highest type of individual and corporate character ; and his ideal of education was a system of culture in which all the requisite forces and factors, intellectual, moral, and spiritual, should be systematically organized to the furtherance of this one result.   Without wide renown or influence, he yet combined a profound penetration and practical judgment with the glad devotion and subduing gentleness of Pestalozzi. The distinguishing vice of educators has always been an overweening confidence in the efficacy of some theoretical method of instruction.   The assumption has been that the perfect method would insure the perfect school and the perfect education.   The great Comenius was a conspicuous offender in this regard, and even the excellent treatise of Milton betrays its author's lack of practical experience in the teaching art by its perpetual lapses into this besetting sin; while the overrated work of Rousseau is little more than the impracticable dream of a conceited enthusiast. It is characteristic of Dr. Muhlenberg that he thought little and wrote less about methods of instruction, while attaching absolute importance to the living spirit of the teacher. Education was not the impartation of knowledge, but the communication of a spirit; not the training of an intelligence, but the development and inspiration of a soul; not the discipline of powers, but the formation of a character; not familiarity with principles, but the perfection of manhood. This is a demand which no method can ever satisfy, — a task for which no method can ever be adequate. Had this great educator's ideal of education been less exalted and noble, he doubtless might have followed in the beaten path of the humdrum schoolteacher. From his own inner consciousness in this case it would have happened that the perfect theory of education — method and all complete — would have been infallibly evolved and given to the world with the glib phraseology of the soul-satisfied vender in educational wares. Another " system " would have been tabulated in the history of pedagogics ; another system-maker would have claimed a niche in the temple of the literary and educational bureau. But this was never his way. Instead of describing the model system of education, as Plato described the model republic, he set about in the most matter-of-fact manner to evolve his model school. Instead of expending his powers in building into symmetry a beautiful and elaborate theory of culture, he set to work to produce the results of true education in the shape of thoroughly developed men. We have seen how much the experiment cost. From the threshold of a life of assured success, and of national if not world-wide fame in his profession, he deliberately consigned himself to years of obscurity and monotonous drudgery, with the grave prospect of very possible failure as his hope of reward in this world. Yet this is the only true method in education. No science of teaching can ever make a school ; no theory of method in teaching can ever develop a character and train a soul, any more than the classifications and analyses of the botanist can construct a flower. Muhlenberg knew that what is wanted first and always is a teacher. And the true teacher will find his own method, which will infallibly be the right one for him. The real teaching force resides in the individuality of the teacher, which the Lord has made and not man, and which is worth more than all the man-made methods in the books. The only stimulating force in the realm of spirit is spirit; the one creative and inspiring agency in the domain of character is character; just as the indispensable condition prerequisite to the development of mind is the presence of other minds. Thus the "method" of Dr. Muhlenberg, in so far as he can be said to have possessed one, was the personal method, — the method of love, of individual interest and personal contact as the moral and spiritual force essential to that rounding of the manhood which is the test of all true education.

In this respect there is but one of the many who have won renown in this great calling with whom he may be justly compared. It would be difficult to lay the finger on a passage in biography at once so touching and so sublime as that in which the heroic Pestalozzi details the simple joys of his passionate self-devotion to the desolate children of the Unter-walden, whom he gathered out of their destitution after the French invasion of 1798 : —

"I was from morning till evening almost alone among them. Everything which was done for their body or soul proceeded from my hand. Every assistance, every help in time of need, every teaching which they received, came immediately from me. My hand lay in their hand, my eye rested on their eye, my tears flowed with theirs, and my laughter accompanied theirs. They were out of the world; they were with me and I was with them. Their soup was mine, their drink was mine. Were they well, I stood in their midst; were they ill, I slept in the middle of them. I was the last who went to bed at night, the first who rose in the morning. Even in bed I prayed and taught with them until they were asleep. They wished it to be so."

Setting aside the adventitious pathos of the great Swiss teacher's situation at that time, arising from the circumstance that these children had been left houseless and parentless, to starve and perish by the accident of war, the words might be taken as a fair and accurate representation of Dr. Muhlenberg's affectionate devotion to the boys of his school. He gave himself wholly to his pupils. The yearning of his heart for them was as strong and true and tender as that of a father for his children. He has been called an apostle to boys; and it is impossible to read the record of his relations with his pupils, to hear the narratives and anecdotes related by those of them still living, without being reminded forcibly of those outpourings of tenderness and expressions of attachment with which St. Paul was wont to speak to the Corinthians and the Philippians. The secret of his power was in

the strong, true love of that Spirit whose out-
goings are recorded in the words of the seven-
teenth chapter of St. John.

The joy of his soul for his dear boys was ever
that joy of the apostle of old when he wrote : —

"I thank my God that in everything ye are enriched by Him in all utterance, and in all knowledge,
so that ye come behind in no gift."

This ulterior aim of developing character in
the pupils settled the type, dominated the administration, and shaped the entire policy of the
school.   In the selection of associates in the
work, the character, spirit, and aim of the teacher
were ever of paramount importance with him.
Whatever the abilities and aptitudes of the individual as a mere instructor, if his influence
and example were not positive and persistent
toward the elevation of the pupils to the plane
of the noblest Christian manhood, he lacked, in
Dr. Muhlenberg's estimation, the essential qualification of a teacher.   He required of his assistants, in the sacred work to which he had consecrated his energies, that they should be men of
like spirit, aims, and ideals with himself.

He could not risk the exposure of the plastic
souls committed to his care beneath the influence of any instructor who esteemed education
as less than a holy calling in the truest sense,

and one involving the weightiest responsibilities. The formation of such an educational staff about him was, of course, the result of a patient process of intelligent selection, and survival of the fittest; and it is no matter of astonishment that, toward the close of this epoch of his life, his corps of assistants was very largely composed of men who had received their education and the bent of their characters from him. The collection and training of such a body of teachers was one of the most important services of his life; for their influence and active labors after his retirement from the work served to perpetuate and determine the type of church school which he originated, whose power and influence and rapidly advancing importance we behold on every side to-day. His method of moral training by personal influence, contact, and example rendered it necessary that the school should be organized and ordered after the pattern of the Christian family. No other type of constitution or administration would have afforded scope and opportunity for that relation of personal intimacy between the teacher and the taught which he esteemed above every other instrumentality in the education of youth. Accordingly master, teachers, and pupils, lived and slept under the same roof, ate from the same table, and felt equally at home in the school family.

The internal régime of the school, both with reference to study and discipline, was extremely simple, natural, and effective. For purposes of discipline, the whole number of boys was divided into sections of twelve. Each section was under the leadership of a " prefect." These prefects were chosen from among the older pupils with reference to their character and qualifications for the work of influencing or restraining those whom they were appointed to lead and control. They were boys of settled habits and determined principles, some of them having the sacred ministry in view ; and yet their position as pupils left them within the range of mutual sympathy between them and their charge, which made their influence effective, because the personal connection was not broken by an impenetrable wall of class separation between the governing and the governed.

In the matter of discipline Dr. Muhlenberg was absolutely independent of any extraneous considerations or control. No pecuniary necessities of the establishment were ever allowed to stand between a pupil of pestilent influence and the dismissal or rigorous discipline demanded by the higher interests of the school. Such cases were rare, of course, yet now and then it was necessary that a corrupting pupil, who had gained an entrance to the school in spite of all precautionary measures, should be dismissed by a severe and peremptory process. It was always clearly understood, however, on receiving a boy, that he was to be returned if for any reason, moral or otherwise, it was deemed better and safer he should not remain. Parental control and authority were always and unconditionally delegated to the rector during term time, which was always so arranged as to include the great church festivals. There was rarely occasion for severity, and never any suggestion of harshness, in the government of the school. The tact and Christian love of the school father, the wisdom of his regulations, the firmness of his will, and the spirit and atmosphere of the establishment, were such as gave to the school the character of a well-ordered Christian household where discipline was rarely needed, because obedience and love were the habit and temper of the common life.

In the department of intellectual culture, his fidelity was in no respect inferior to that displayed in point of discipline or moral training. Although regarding religion as the flower and fruit of culture, and of paramount importance in the development of character, yet it was one of his maxims constantly enforced, that " religion should never be held to account for inferior scholarship." The exclusion of emulation as a

motive to exertion in study, was a principle from
which he never departed. Competition for
grade, or a prize in any form, was never allowed.
He entertained the firm conviction that such a
method and such motives were damaging to
character. Emulation he considered evil in its
influence, and incapable of being employed to
any salutary end in education. As an incentive
he held it to be an unhealthful stimulant, and
injurious to the moral principle.

The religious culture and influence of the
school was a unique and triumphant achievement of Dr. Muhlenberg as an educator. When
one thinks of the dreary, dead perfunctoriness
of the ordinary American college chapel service,
with its stereotyped formalism, and its stale, un-
profitable monotony, one is filled with an instantaneous impulse of thankfulness for the spiritual
genius who permanently succeeded in making
attractive and helpful to all what had always before been regarded, by the average youth, with
instinctive aversion and dislike. The enthusiasm with which surviving " College Pointers "
detail their recollections of these exercises is
equaled only by their affectionate tributes to
the memory of Dr. Muhlenberg. It was the
pervading effect of their master's personality,
indeed, that lent one great element of attraction
to these services. His impressive presence, the

simple force and naturalness of his noble manner and bearing, imparted an inevitable charm to everything he did. But the style of service which he instituted had a power peculiarly its own, independently of any personal influence or accidental circumstance. Dr. Muhlenberg was a genuine poet, and the chapel observance was the realized action of the divine poetry inherent in Christian truth and the spirit of worship. He has been variously regarded by diverse factions in his own communion as the Coryphæus of extreme ritual practice in this country from his having come under the spell of the Puseyite or Oxford movement of that day. No imputation was ever more absurd ; no intended compliment was ever so untrue to fact, while at the same time ignoring the real originality and merit of the service which it was designed to exalt. Years before the Oxford movement had excited a ripple on the Dead Sea of that supercilious self-complacency which Anglican sacramentalism had presented for two hundred years, a full decade before Evangelicalism had been roused from its dogmatic slumbers to the pitch of sudden frenzy by the Oxford heresy, the services at Flushing Institute were conducted on a basis of elaborate and varied ritual, and ornamented with all the adjuncts of the most advanced requirements. The difference between the Oxford rit-

ual and that at the school in Long Island was,
that the latter was directed by a man of too
catholic a temper to admit of ever being wedded
to any abstract theory as to its significance, or of
being tied to any routine of unvarying form. To
use his own words, " The ritualism we practiced
was certainly not of the Romish type, but the
product of imagination in accordance with the
verities of our religion." " Everything tended,"
says one of his school sons,[1] " in the service of the
chapel, to bring out the religion of the heart."
And the venerated school father, with his poet's
soul, understood the human heart well enough to
know that it would not grow its religion from a
dry bulb. The religion of the heart is not of the
naked cactus kind that is evolved from desert
sand, but a product adorned with every grace
and beauty of form, and enriched with all the
varied charms of foliage and flower. He viewed
human nature in its complexity, and with the
genius of a King David or a St. Gregory he saw
that the religion of the chapel, as of the temple,
must not be a bare stock on a wintry moorland,
but a luxuriant plant, in full tropical magnifi-
cence of bloom, beneath the radiance of heaven's
most joyous and benignant light. And because
the living soul of the poet would not suffer the
form to become stereotyped and changeless, so

---

[1] The Rev. Ormes B. Keith, in a private letter.

that a prosaic interpretation might be forced
upon it, no alarm was felt for his influence or
example in the matter. What these chapel exercises were, is best related in the words of one
who was associated with him in different capaci-
ties, as boy and man, during all the years of his
educational career : [1] —

"The chapel services incited every mind to holy
thought and every heart to virtuous desire. There
the father ministered as at a family altar. He was
always the father, though clad in priestly vestment.
Those services were seldom forgotten by those who
once felt their blessed influence. They were strictly
churchly, though not after any stereotyped formula.
Men of mature years and old men have told me that
the memory of these chapel services held them
through life firm to the gospel of Jesus ; that sweet
ritual observance, genuine Christian ritualism, with
incense and lights, with pictures and flowers, kept
them loyal to the church. There was nothing perfunctory : every word and act were real, true to the
spirit of that Protestant Evangelical Churchmanship
which is the tower of strength, the sure refuge of
gospel faith. Matins, vespers, and a brief noonday
service, attendance upon which was voluntary, made
up the worship of every day. The impressive reading of Holy Scripture, the solemn chanting of Psalms,
the fervent intercessions, often fresh from the father's

[1] The Rev. Libertus Van Bokkelen, D. D., in *The Churchman.*

heart, the litanies selected from ancient missals and adapted to special seasons, made it a privilege and pleasure to go to the oratory and be there with God.

"Each holy day was observed, not only in chapel services, but in the routine of academic exercises. Christmas and Easter were gorgeous festivals. Holy Week was holy indeed, with penitential confessions and prayers; its solemn *Miserere* culminating in the impressive office of Good Friday, when the altar was vested with black, and over it hung the picture of the crucifixion.

"Thus many a young rebellious spirit was softened, bound by the cords of love; many a heart awakened to earnest love and adoration of the Lamb of God who taketh away the sins of the world, or as it was sung, *Agnus Dei qui peccata mundi tollis, miserere nobis.*

"Seasons of joy were the Feasts of the Nativity and Resurrection. Then the chapel was brilliant and fragrant. The altar wore its vestment of white and shone with lights. There was the picture of the Madonna wreathed with evergreens, surrounded by flowers exhaling fragrance as incense to the Lord. This was the beginning and the perfection of æsthetic ritualism. There was no school vacation at Christmas and Easter, no scattering of the school family. The spiritual father kept his spiritual children by his side, and good was it for them that so he did. It gave reality to his ministrations, and left a life-long benediction upon all who thus learned to worship God in the beauty of holiness. The potency of the teachings in chapel, in family worship, and in voluntary meeting was in the one word JESUS, the name above every name, — Jesus, the perfection and the power of the Divine Love. . . . If ever Jesus was in an earthly home, all in all, his teachings the inspiration, his example the rule, it was in that home where William Augustus Muhlenberg, the apostle to the young, fed the lambs of Christ's flock.

"These chapel services, as has been said, antedated that general revival of ritual which came with the teaching of Keble's "Christian Year," when the Flushing Institute was the only true Christian family school of our church, when Lent was not kept with daily prayer, and when Christmas was a day of merry-making. Thus the school at Flushing was a teacher of the whole church. Seed was then sown of which we are now reaping a rich and blessed harvest. Honor to him who began the good work, in which thousands now rejoice, when church schools are in every diocese, and Christian teaching is yielding abundant fruit, to the glory of God and for the kingdom of his dear Son."

It is impossible at this late date to reproduce one of these school services, for they varied in character, and were all hinged upon the personality of the master mind which presided over them. But the parent at St. Paul's School, Concord, who has felt the wonderful influence of the Coit brothers there, in the growing character and forming habits of his boy who has been left to their eminently wise and tender care, can see, in these peculiarly " tender Shepherd " ministrations, the spirit of Him who taught these teachers, and can catch something of what these school services must have been.

The extent and effect of Dr. Muhlenberg's personal labors for the individual religious welfare of his pupils can never be estimated. In this direction his efforts and influence were untiring and most effective. This was the supreme aim of all his toil and striving, the development and discipline of a genuinely Christian character and temper in his boys. But from the nature of such personal work, its methods and results must continue unknown. The fragmentary vestiges and isolated reminiscences that yet remain of his work in this direction afford ample evidence, however, of the personal interest with which he watched, and strove, and prayed for the spiritual welfare of each individual pupil, as well as the deep and true affection with which his heart went out towards every boy entrusted to his care and keeping. As his acquaintance with each one grew, and his interest in him increased, his manner, while it never repelled by any exuberant demonstrations, nevertheless made itself felt by the recipient as the unfeigned expression of an almost parental tenderness. The religious life was, in his view, but one aspect of the man, one pervading and inseparable element of the completed character; and therefore the method by which he endeavored to awaken and cultivate the religious principle in youth was the same as that by which he strove to develop manhood in them; it was the personal method. In doing the work of the Master he pursued the method of the Master, because he had the spirit of the Master, — the spirit that sought out the young man whom the Jews had put out of the synagogue for being healed of his blindness, and revealed to him the secret of his mission; the spirit that looked on the rich young man and loved him; that quietly said to Judas, without a look or tone or syllable of harshness, "What thou doest, do quickly;" that sent the personal message, "Go tell my disciples and Peter;" that patiently convinced the despondent Thomas, — "Reach hither thy finger and behold my hand, and reach hither thy hand and thrust it into my side, and be not faithless but believing." He made himself the servant of each for Jesus' sake, in the conviction that human characters are saved and nurtured only by immediate personal contact and sympathy in the fellowship of love.

Many a pupil of his, who grew to large usefulness and high eminence in Christian character, owed his first inspiration to the holy example and affectionate, faithful words of his preceptor, uttered in private, with all his own inimitable naturalness and earnest solicitude. More than one such has told the writer of the doctor's warm embrace, and tearful words of sympathy, in some sad hour of parting or of grief.

Yet he was ever bubbling over with the most genial and sparkling humor. None knew better than he how effective a weapon humor is in the management of boys, and none knew better how to use it. The anecdotes of his felicitous repartees and droll sayings are numberless. A single instance, selected for its brevity, must here suffice.

The clerical members of the faculty at college were accustomed to take turns at preaching in the Sunday afternoon services. The young man who had charge of the chapel music, on going one Sunday to the rector for the hymns to be used that afternoon, was asked whose turn it was to preach. At the mention of the name the doctor, turning quickly with a merry twinkle in his eye, replied, "Now I lay me down to sleep."

His power over these young lives, and his success in moulding them to something of his own ideal of character, were the fruit of a very close and well-kept Christian life. Like the turbine in the wheel-pit, the sources of his power were hidden, yet they streamed in on him from above. The outside world saw only the swift and glistening machinery of his outward life, or admired its finished product; but now and then a friend would get a casual glimpse of the ponderous wheels, far down in the secret depths of his being, which moved it all, as they themselves were moved, by the strong currents of Divine impulsion. The stern vigilance of self which he continually employed; the silent hours of meditation, prayer, and fellowship with Jesus, by which he kept the fountains of his loving energy continually fresh and running over, — can be guessed at only from a perusal of his private journal.

Such were a few of the leading lines of his method and some of his distinguishing characteristics as an educator. In thus analyzing his work we have been studying the source of one of the most beneficent influences in Christian education. In that great movement toward making education distinctly Christian, which is rapidly assuming national proportions, he was unquestionably the pioneer; he saw the movement well under way and assured of ultimate success before he withdrew personally from the work. During the years of his experiment at Flushing and College Point, church schools, under the stimulus of his ideas, example, and success, rapidly

became the fashion. Indeed, it was one of the
evils incident to the novel character of the work,
that the number of schools grew more rapidly
than was consistent with the high standard he
had set. Teachers with the requisite qualifications for the kind of work could not be obtained
in sufficient numbers. He was besieged with
applications, by bishops of the church and others
who were founding similar schools, for teachers
trained by himself. In a letter to Bishop
Whittingham, of Maryland, rēgretting his in-
ability to furnish a classical teacher whom the
bishop had begged him to send, he declared:
" Almost every week I am making the same
reply to similar applications. Teachers for
church schools are now the demand everywhere,
and of the right kind they are not to be found."
He had previously, however (1841), in response
to the bishop's importunity, consented to give
up his trusted assistant and right-hand man at
College Point, — the Rev. J. B. Kerfoot, afterwards first Bishop of Pittsburgh, — in order to
insure the successful inauguration of St. James'
Hall — afterwards the College of St. James —
in accordance with Dr. Muhlenberg's principles
and methods. The thrilling story of this institution and its relation to St. Paul's, College
Point, has been inimitably told by the Rev. Hall
Harrison, in his very interesting and masterly

biography of Bishop Kerfoot. Both St. Paul's and St. James' are now no more; but "the work of Dr. Muhlenberg, and of St. James' College modified and in many ways improved, yet, after all, essentially the same, took a new start, and still lives at St. Paul's School, Concord, New Hampshire. For it was his friendship with Kerfoot and his observation of the actual working of St. James' that first inspired that most helpful layman of Massachusetts, Dr. George C. Shattuck, of Boston, with the thought of founding a similar school for the church in New England. He secured for its head one who had been both a disciple of Dr. Muhlenberg's and an associate of Kerfoot in the College of St. James, — the Rev. Henry Augustus Coit, who, working with his brother the vice-rector, also a St. James man, has made St. Paul's what it is to-day, the most famous of all our church schools." [1]

Thus the Muhlenberg ideal in education has easily maintained its prerogative of leadership and commanding influence over all schools of its type, through successive institutions and epochs from the time of its origin to our own.

Dr. Muhlenberg's service as a leader in the cause of Christian education was twofold: first, in awakening a general interest in the public mind upon the subject; and secondly, in illus-

[1] *Life of Bishop Kerfoot*, vol. i. pp. 47, 48.

trating by his own practical experiment the true method and aim of all education. It is difficult for us at this distant day to realize how conspicuous his service was in the first of these particulars, and how crying was the need of it. Within his own communion, church schools were unknown. Such schools as did exist were private enterprises on a purely business or pecuniary and secular basis. Education was never dreamed of as a sacred calling to be controlled by the loftiest ideals, and demanding the most thorough and responsible oversight of the church. But through eighteen years of consecrated personal toil Dr. Muhlenberg wrought a complete educational reformation within his own branch of the church. Church schools of the type conceived by him sprang up on every hand, and have continued to multiply with unabated rapidity and increasing success down to the present time. The whole subsequent educational movement and life of the church was inaugurated by him, and is as distinctly traceable to him as the historic river Rhine is traceable to the little lake in the Splügen Pass from which it has its source. And this result he achieved, not by noisy agitation, but by the force of quiet example and patient experiment. A firm believer in organic or institutional Christianity, he was convinced that the office of the Christian church is not merely to evangelize, but also to educate in every highest and best sense of the word; and that this latter function of the church is more laborious, and more persistent in its demands, than the other.

This conviction is now rapidly becoming universal, as the schools at Concord, Groton, and Southborough, testify. The other contribution by which he placed the educational world under obligation to him was of a more general character, and more decidedly original. It is quite safe to affirm that the prevalent ideal before Dr. Muhlenberg's day, with regard to the aim of education, was generically different from that which he enunciated. The object of education, as popularly conceived among us, was intellectual, as distinguished from a moral or spiritual result. That totality of the man which we term character was not taken into the account in framing the popular ideal of the end of education. The moral and spiritual elements of the individual organization were disregarded in making up the estimate of a finished education, being looked upon rather as separate compartments which might be fitted up for use on Sundays in church or elsewhere, but with which education, properly speaking, had nothing to do. It had relation only or chiefly to the intelligence, to the development and training of the

intellectual faculty. To Dr. Muhlenberg's influence, more than to any other American, is
due the fact that this false ideal has been grad-
ually revolutionized, or rather has been sup-
planted by the opposite conception, which is
destined at no distant day to work a signal
transformation of our whole educational system
and machinery.

As to the method by which the true end of
education is to be reached, his example will
ever remain much more valuable even than the
manner of his technique. The spiritual insight
and instinct which led him to expect compara-
tively little result from the mere inculcation of
abstract principles or concrete facts, and to at-
tach supreme importance to the individuality
and personal influence of the teacher, reveal the
genius of the true educator. His was the
method of the Divine Teacher. Having the
perfection of character as the ideal end of education, he perceived with the intuitive glance of
the seer that character could not be formed by
precept, rule, and dogma, but only by its exem-
plification in the daily and hourly relation of
the teacher with the taught; in other words, by
incarnating and transfusing the spirit of love by
means of all the manners, tempers, words, and
actions of the teacher's life.

"God has conceded two sights to a man:
  One of men's whole work, Time's completed plan;
  The other of the minutest work, man's first
  Step to the plan's completeness: what's dispersed
  Save hope of that supreme step which, descried
  Earliest, was meant still to remain untried
  Only to give you heart to take your own
  Step and there stay — leaving the rest alone?"

ROBERT BROWNING, *Sordello.*

THE TYPE OF CHURCHMANSHIP
OF WHICH MUHLENBERG
WAS THE CREATOR.

"St. Bernard has said: 'Man, if thou desirest a noble and holy life, and unceasingly prayest to God for it, if thou continue constant in this thy desire, it will be granted unto thee without fail, even if only at the day and hour of thy death; and if God should not give it to thee then, thou shalt find it in Him in eternity: of this be assured.' Therefore do not relinquish your desire, though it be not fulfilled immediately, or though you may swerve from your aspirations, or even forget them for a time. . . . The love and aspiration which once really existed live forever before God, and in Him ye shall find the fruit thereof; that is, to all eternity it shall be better for you than if you had never felt them." — J. TAULER.

"That which befits us, embosomed in beauty and wonder as we are, is cheerfulness, and courage, and the endeavor to realize our aspirations. Shall not the heart, which has received so much, trust the Power by which it lives? May it not quit other leadings, and listen to the Soul that has guided it so gently, and taught it so much, secure that the future will be worthy of the past?" — R. W. EMERSON.

CHAPTER III.

THE TYPE OF CHURCHMANSHIP OF WHICH MUHLENBERG WAS THE CREATOR.

THE axiomatic couplet of one of Tennyson's famous verses in his " In Memoriam " contains the well-known words : —

> " So careful of the type she seems,
> So careless of the single life."

Nature does indeed preserve the type. We see the type face, the type life, and the type thought and habit of mind. That which once becomes established in the type or mould maintains itself with the persistent strength of the habitude of chronic survival. And in this way we find that, according to the working of this common law, the types of churchmanship which prevail to-day are the types which the historian finds at Alexandria with Clement, or at Carthage with Cyprian or Tertullian, or at Constantinople with Chrysostom. This fact explains much of our typical American churchmanship to-day, and illustrates the mission of the church for the future. The problem to-day is that

of making useful and full of power the rich
inheritance of knowledge and experience be-
queathed to the church by its forefathers.   The
American Episcopal Church is like a dear old
homestead which has been full of life and activity, and is to-day filled with many memories.
Brothers and sisters have been reared in it, and
have gone forth to make varying alliances and
to accomplish many widespread and opposite results in the outer world.   Back from the world's
ever-widening broad way it stands ; yet its ancient gateway leads directly to the highway of
modern thought and life.   It speaks to us, by
its antique structure, of bygone methods of architecture ; yet where can one find such solid
comfort in any of the new-fashioned homes of
to-day ?   It speaks, by its whole air of yesterday, of the wisdom and experience of the past ;
but the inmates of the old homestead are young
and active children of the present.   The belong-
ings of bygone relatives are found here, — the
silver, the furniture, the pictures, and the dra-
peries of the generations that have lived in it, —
but the methods of the present householders are
the methods of to - day.   In other words, this
church in this new land of ours has inherited
the wisdom and experience of those who helped
to make it what it is, and who builded better
than they knew.   While other forms of faith

are perishing at the first hard conflict of bygone methods with new-found experiences, it is living unharmed and unscathed, because its fathers struggled to have in the homestead room enough for a very large family of very active children.

I.

It is of churchmanship that we are to speak in the present chapter, and as a churchman Dr. Muhlenberg was *sui generis*. The immediate impulse of dominant partisans, whether of the ecclesiastical or scientific type, is to classify under existing formulæ every fresh individual who comes within the sphere of their observation. In this way it comes to pass that whenever any eager spirit ventures upon a thing so daring as the declaration of personal convictions, the novel specimen is forthwith seized upon by the learned and dignified fraternity that lies in wait, and is calmly impaled on the walls of their cabinet under his appropriate label, where, stripped of every semblance of life and spontaneous vigor, and with everything distinctive in his composition ready to crumble at the touch of a living finger, he is exhibited for the instruction of successive generations. To succeed in thus pinning a new spiritual leader to a neat bit of cardboard in a glass case, and labeled with a familiar or a high-sounding name, is to consign him to that limbo wherein, it is conceived, he will have no longer

any power to deceive the nations. Dr. Muhlenberg, with the prerogative that belongs to all
genius, and most of all to spiritual genius, uni-
formly set at naught, and brought to untimely
ridicule, all such artificial attempts to formulate
him. When the ecclesiastical experts had se-
curely pinned him down to the Church of the
Holy Communion as a sort of chrysalid " Puseyite," emerging from the cocoon of the " Oxford
Movement," he suddenly spread his hitherto
hidden wings and soared away into regions of
catholic liberty and evangelical truth, whither
their lesser powers of vision could not follow
him. In this way, also, when others began to
speak of him as nothing more than a commonplace Lutheran, who in being educated into the
church had not been educated out of the æsthetic symbolism in worship which the Church
of the Fatherland has never renounced, their
theory was confronted with the ill-fitting fact that
he was a champion of the episcopate, and a radical exponent of episcopal prerogative, the like
of whom, not even excepting Bishop John Henry
Hobart, had not arisen on either side of the Atlantic for more than a hundred years. Dr.
Muhlenberg persistently defied all efforts to
classify him in terms of existing ecclesiastical
nomenclature ; and by way of inventing one for
himself that would sufficiently indicate his position, he gave to the Christian world a term which

ought to elicit the loyal confession, and awaken
the ardent enthusiasm, of every churchman and
every believing Christian. He proclaimed himself an " Evangelical Catholic." His own definition of this term, as drawn out in the fullest
and clearest manner in a letter to a friend, has
since been given to the public by the author of
his memoir. This letter, notwithstanding its
great merit, is too long to be quoted in the present volume.

Dr. Muhlenberg, as this remarkable letter
shows, was not afraid of the term " Catholic,"
nor yet of its opposite, the word " Evangelical."
But he strove most zealously and conscientiously
to strip each of these expressions of the unconscious " cant " which was hidden in them, which
wrong usage had laid them open to the bias of
party pride and prejudice.

In this respect he resembled his great English fellow-churchman, Maurice, who was always
radical in thought and conservative in expression, and the great New England theologian and
Puritan divine, Dr. Bushnell, of Hartford. Unlike Maurice and Bushnell in that he did not
profess to be a theologian, he was yet like them
in their delightful element of practical largeness
of vision and grasp of opposing phases of truth.

He perceived what the so - called Catholic
Churchman was striving for, and he realized the

power of the justification-by-faith position of
the Low Church Calvinistic school; and feeling
as he did that the genius of the Episcopate
reached as far east as it did west, he constantly
strove to keep the feet of all the church's clergy
in a large room, where the sect spirit and the
crack of the partisan's whip would forever be at
a discount.

The result of this was, that he was blamed
by each wing of the church while living, though
now that he is dead, both schools of thought rejoice in his influence, and honor him for his potent
comprehensiveness.   His definition of Evangelical Catholicism, contained in the letter referred
to, was occasioned by the publication and establishment, under Dr. Muhlenberg's auspices, of
a journal entitled "The Evangelical Catholic,"
devoted to the exposition of what he conceived to
be the Catholic and Apostolic idea of the Church
of Christ.   The appearance of this modest sheet
was the occasion of no little surprise, owing to
the very wide divergence of views maintained in
it from all the partisan positions which Dr.
Muhlenberg was supposed to have espoused.
He was no "Puseyite," he was a Catholic Christian, and a Catholic in a sense calculated and
destined to redeem the word from the restricted
monopoly of use which had been arrogated for
so many centuries by the Papal See.   So far was

he from being an adherent of the Oxford school, that he had never even accepted the doctrine of baptismal regeneration, which was the corner-stone of their theological structure. What Dr. Muhlenberg meant by Evangelical Catholicism in reference to matters of faith and doctrine has been sufficiently set forth in the letter re-ferred to. It now remains to represent the prin-ciples of Evangelical Catholicism as illustrated by his conception of their proper application to the practical affairs of church administration and worship.

First of all, with reference to the work for which the Church of Christ is ordained in the world, Dr. Muhlenberg held that the church is essentially and supremely a missionary organiza-tion. Primarily and in essence she is evangelic. The great end of her existence is the preaching of the gospel, the delivery of God's message to the world. She has no restricted mission. Her commission reaches to all sorts and conditions of men, and her obligation to fulfill it to the in-clusion of all is unqualified. To this end every-thing must be subordinated ; in order to the realization of this high purpose, her entire sys-tem and machinery must be flexible and easy of adaptation. Whatever of human enactment hinders or obstructs this is, *ipso facto*, null and void.

Secondly, in the due order and regulation of this divinely ordained function the church is Catholic. In her duly commissioned ministry, in the freedom, the rites, and the regulation of her worship, as well as in the unity of her faith, the church is Catholic. The oversight of the church, and especially the commissioning of her ministers by bishops as the successors of the apostles,[1] is of primitive and universal order in the Church of Christ. Whether such order of bishops be of apostolic institution, is a question that has no bearing, so long as no other origin is satisfactorily proven, or as long as the order cannot be shown to be in itself a hindrance to the preaching of the gospel. The freedom of prayer and of prophesying, and the right of all the people of the congregation to participate actively and audibly in the stated exercises of public worship in the sanctuary, are points of Catholic liberty, incident to the fellowship of the Holy Ghost, which the Catholic Church can never surrender. To proscribe freedom of prayer and prophesying, within orderly limitations, is to be unevangelical; to deny the use of liturgic forms, under due restriction and control, as a means of participation by the people in the acts of public worship and of voicing their common prayer, is to be uncatholic.

[1] " In order if not in office." — (W. H. M.)

It is not a matter of present concern to the writer or the public that these principles be defended or controverted, but that they be shown to be the views entertained by Dr. Muhlenberg. Recourse shall therefore be had to his own words, written in explanation of that movement which is the subject of the succeeding chapter in this book.

(1.)

THE GREAT COMMISSION OF THE CHURCH.

" That paper (the Memorial), however, was not addressed to the members of the church at large, nor to their representatives in General Convention, but solely to the Right Reverend the Fathers of the Church. And it is for them to say whether, with such an answer,[1] or any approximation to it, they will dismiss the memorialists. It is for them to say whether they believe, what such an answer implies, that they are the bishops of a church with a restricted mission. It is for them to say whether they believe that their episcopate has its full scope when limited to a field of action which does not embrace all sorts and conditions of men, nor is ever likely to embrace them. Remembering their broad commission from the great Head of the Church, are they satisfied that they are executing it while limited to a society or communion which so

[1] He had been stating the answer to the Memorial of those who, while acknowledging the inadequacy of the church to the wants of the age, yet maintained that she was serving the gospel sufficiently in her appointed sphere as one in the sisterhood of Protestant sects.

far lacks catholicity that, from some inherent fault of its own, it is incompetent to evangelize the world around it? Of course they are not. They would repudiate so narrow a view of their functions: they cannot look upon themselves as no more than the executive officers of one of the many societies of Protestantism, and that, too, an inferior one in numbers and powers of increase. They recognize in their office all that is implied in the office of bishops in and of the Catholic Church of Christ.[1] . . . The course now to be considered contemplates action solely on the part of bishops. It proposes that, for the discharge of their office chiefly in admitting to the sacred ministry, they shall enlarge their borders; that they shall mark out for their action as bishops some broader and more catholic ground than that to which they are now restricted. This, while it is obviously the safer policy in regard to the interests of the Protestant Episcopal Church as such, gives wider scope to the bishops than probably would ever be afforded by any modification of her system. It puts her in no jeopardy. It need not alarm her most conservative friends. It says, Let her boundaries stand; let everything in them remain in *statu quo*, if that be desired, but let not the word of the Lord be bound. Let it 'have free course, and be glorified.' Let those who are charged with its propagation over the world have the full liberty in sending forth its preachers. Let their power to this effect be recognized even beyond what is provided for by the laws and regulations of our particular com-

[1] *Evangelical Catholic Papers*, First Series, pp. 112, 113.

munion, — not in contrariety to those laws and regulations, not to violate either their letter or their spirit,
not to interfere with them in any way, and yet not
in pursuance of them, not in virtue of their authority.
By what authority then, it is asked, may our bishops
act in the premises contemplated, if they have it not
from the Protestant Episcopal Church? Where is
their warrant for doing what her canons do not contemplate their doing? Are we to have the doctrine
of a Higher Law? 'Even so a Higher Law.' 'Go
ye into all the world and preach the gospel to every
creature.'[1] . . . 'They, then, who are required by
that (primitive and universal) order, or who in virtue
of it have an unquestioned right to commission men to
preach the gospel (viz., the bishops), are eminently
bound to do so. To them as to no others comes the
voice of the Lord in unbroken accents along the current of centuries, 'Go ye into all the world.' To this
both High and Low Churchmen assent; but setting
antiquity aside, making no account of the historical
episcopate, nor saying what the succession is worth,
take the fact as it now stands, — take only what is
patent and present. The bishops, and the bishops
only, can give a commission to preach the gospel
which obtains credit everywhere in the Protestant
world. This or that denomination of Christians may
be perfectly sure that a commission from other hands
is quite as good, but there is no common consent to
that effect. Episcopal orders alone have a universal
currency. Upon those, then, who have it in their

[1] *Evangelical Catholic Papers*, First Series, pp. 117, 118.

power, lies the bounden duty to dispense such orders.
The possession of a gift involves the obligation to use
it to the utmost good.[1] 'Necessity is laid upon me,
. . . woe is me if I preach not the gospel,' cried one
in the apostolic episcopate. Let those in the episcopate now feel that a like necessity is laid upon them.
Let them feel constrained to the preaching of the
gospel by sending forth all they can whom they believe to be qualified to preach it, and their invention
will not fail them in devising how to do it, and that
without their abating a jot or tittle of their present
ecclesiastical allegiance. Let it only become in earnest
a problem for the episcopal college, and who doubts its
solution?[2] If there be any law or rule of the Protestant Episcopal Church confining them within her own
range, it is null and void. It abridges their original
commission. It trenches on their inherent powers.
It contravenes the Higher Law. But there is none.
The Protestant Episcopal Church has no occasion to
contemplate episcopal action outside of herself. It
does not come within her province : accordingly she
does not legislate for it.[3] When a bishop says his
hands are tied so that he dare not lay them upon any
one who will not step upon the Protestant Episcopal
platform and promise never to leave it, he might be
well asked, what has tied them? Is it the original
commission? Is it a word or syllable in that commission? That will not be pretended. Is it ancient and
universal precedent? Neither will that be said. Is it

[1] *Evangelical Catholic Papers*, First Series, pp. 120, 121.
[2] *Ibid.*, p. 139.   [3] *Ibid.*, pp. 122, 123.

the necessity of security for the Catholic faith? That much security let him demand. But the Protestant Episcopal Church has tied his hands. How so? She engaged him most solemnly, indeed, to conformity to her doctrine, discipline, and worship, and that binds him irrevocably in his relations to her; but does she anywhere say that he shall have no other relations? Did he, could he, promise to have no other? The oath of allegiance to the Protestant Episcopal Church binds him in everything with which that allegiance is concerned, — it binds him acting with and for the Protestant Episcopal Church, — but has he so far given up his freedom in Christ, has he so contracted his Christian charity, as to have engaged never to act among others, or for others, in doing them good, provided that in so doing he occasion no detriment to his own communion? He swore to do his duty within her bounds after the manner which she prescribes, but did he forswear all episcopal duty beyond her bounds? This is at least a question, and, if a question at all, a very grave one. Let it be resolved by those whom it most intimately concerns. If they deem themselves incompetent to its solution, let it be brought before the general council of the church. Let the question, with its momentous bearings, be pressed upon the members of that body in some form that will test their convictions upon it. Let them deliberately say whether they believe that the episcopal office, which most if not all of them believe to be a divine institution for spreading the means of salvation, may not be exercised except within the limits of their own appointment, and according to laws and regulations of their own enactment. Let them pray at the opening of each day's session the prayer, 'that the comfortable Gospel of Christ may be truly preached, truly received, and truly followed in all places,' and then vote that, so far as in them lies, the comfortable Gospel of Christ shall not be preached save with the coextension of their own particular ecclesiastical system. Let them pray that 'the whole of Christ's sheep may be gathered into one fold,' and then vote in effect that the 'one fold' is the Protestant Episcopal fold : let them so vote, and then deny, with what consistency they can, that they are in the bondage of sect." [1]

(2.)

Episcopal Freedom.

"The central idea of the movement, as contemplated in the wider aim of the Memorial, is the emancipation of the Protestant Episcopate : upon this it all turns. As for the Roman Episcopate, it is in hopeless vassalage to the Italian Pontiff. The Reformation on the continent of Europe did not effect its deliverance. The bishops there continued the abject servants of the Pope. The new-born spirit of the times, invoking them to assert their freedom, did

[1] The convention virtually has already done this in setting forth a translation of the Prayer Book in the German language, for the purpose of enabling such of our ministers as are qualified to preach the gospel to German emigrants. Most of these people have already the creed, the psalms, and part of our service in their books of devotion. Why was not that sufficient ? *Evangelical Catholic Papers*, First Series, pp. 187, 188.

not reach their wills, and they still hugged their chains.

"But the gospel was no longer in chains: they had burst asunder at the voice of the Lord, and the voice of the Lord, 'mighty in operation,' was now summoning all, laymen, priests, and bishops alike, to the 'liberty wherewith Christ hath made us free.' If the bishops choose to remain in bondage (in effect said the arch-reformer), so let them, but not we. Whatever allegiance we owe them, since it binds us to allegiance to the Pope, we break it, as we must, for the sake of allegiance to our sovereign Lord Christ. And break it they did; but never, by so doing, did the thought ever enter their minds that they broke away from the Church of Christ. Though they parted from the bishops, they felt that they did not part from the Bishop and Shepherd of souls, and so could not be out of his fold. *Ubi Christus, ibi Ecclesia,* was the creed of their churchmanship: we need not examine its soundness. The question of the integrity of the reformed churches, thus deprived by necessity of the episcopate, is one with which we are not now concerned. As one of the memorialists, I waive it. I have a settled opinion upon it, but the present argument does not call for its expression. It is wide of its scope. Its decision is unnecessary, for happily in the providence of God, the episcopate in England did sever itself from the Papacy. The English bishops so far became free, and yet not free. They found themselves in another bondage. Prelates in allegiance with the state, they were restrained in their office as the bishops of

Christ, — they were not free to exercise it solely in obedience to Christ. Among the facts in evidence of that, there was a remarkable one in our own history. The English bishops dared not convey the Episcopal functions to their American brethren suing for them, without the leave of the civil power. An act of parliament was necessary in order to empower them to perpetuate, beyond their own shores, a commission which, under divine obligations, they were thus bound to perpetuate. Practically they were as dependent upon his Majesty George III. as any Roman bishops in like case would be now on his Holiness Pius IX. They got leave. Most gladly did they use it, and now through them we have bishops dependent on neither pope nor king; nevertheless, — with unfeigned deference I say it, — bishops in bondage still. The thraldom of the Papacy has forever passed away. The thraldom of the state has never been imposed, but the thraldom of sect remains. For how else shall that be designated which denies them a catholic freedom in the highest function of their office; which limits them, not by the necessary economy of jurisdiction, but by conventional restrictions, far within the range of the Catholic faith and of human appointment? Beyond these they dare not go, and within these every one, to have the benefit of their office, must come, and moreover bind himself to remain. Neither they who have the power to grant, nor they who accept from them the commission to preach Christ's gospel, may exceed a particular platform, — that of the Protestant Episcopal Communion. They may carry forward that platform; they may plant it wherever they can; and such an extension of it is the end they are to aim at, — it is their set limit of action. In other words, the bishops are bound to the propagation exclusively of Protestant Episcopalianism. They are denied the liberty of spreading the gospel under any other form, — and that, sure, is to be in bondage. Let us turn to the original and divine commission in the premises, on which all depends.

" ' All power is given unto me in heaven and earth; go ye therefore and teach all nations, baptizing them in the name of the Father, and of the Son, and of the Holy Ghost; teaching them to observe all things whatsoever I have commanded you, and lo, I am with you alway, even unto the end of the world.' So we read in St. Matthew. St. Mark has the same in somewhat different language: ' Go ye unto all the world and preach the gospel to every creature. He that believeth and is baptized shall be saved; but he that believeth not shall be damned.'

" Here is plainly declared the purpose for which Christ sent forth his apostles. The same must have been the purpose for which they sent forth others after them. The same must be that of every successor of the apostles in sending forth men to the end of time. They must adhere to it unchanged. If they add any secondary purpose to it, it must be altogether in harmony with it; it must be no let or hindrance to it, else they incur a forfeiture of the promise of his being with them to the end of the world.

"Now what was and what is that purpose? It
lies open on the face of the commission. It is none
other than this, — that all men should hear the gospel; that all men should be taught the gospel; that
all who believed should be baptized in the name of the
Father, and of the Son, and of the Holy Ghost, and
consequently should be taught to believe in, to worship, love, and obey the Father, the Son, and the
Holy Ghost; further, that they should be taught to
observe all things whatsoever Christ commanded his
disciples, and which are found written in the New
Testament. Whenever, then, a bishop is satisfied
that a Christian man of sound mind, asking of him
the ministerial commission, will so preach and teach,
will so baptize them in the name of the Blessed
Trinity, and consequently inculcate upon them obedience and love to the three Persons and one God, in
their several relations to man and in their essential
unity, and further will instruct those who believe in
the will of Christ contained in his word, the bishop
is free to give the commission, — nothing may hinder.
Canons, custom, or usages, if they are in the way, are
to be scattered as chaff before the wind. They are
impertinences coming between the mouth of the Lord
and the will of his servant. They are checks and hold-
backs, when the word of the Lord is, Go forward. This
is the doctrine of Episcopal freedom in the abstract.
In practice, of course, it calls for law, rule, discipline,
for the purpose of its effectual exercise. Order being
' Heaven's first law,' Episcopal freedom cannot be superior to it. Bishops must be subject to order, else

there will be confusion among them. They will interfere with one another, — the gospel will be hindered,
not furthered. This is obvious. There must be order, — just so much order, however, as is necessary
to the furtherance of the gospel; just so much as ex-
pedites the fulfillment of the evangelical command." [1]

The following letter to the Rev. J. B. Kerfoot, Bishop-elect of Pittsburgh, dated Decem-
ber, 1865, will serve to complete these citations
relative to the mission of the church and the
prerogative of her bishops : —

"My dear John, — You ask me to be present
at your consecration. With all the love I bear you,
I can hardly think of undertaking such a journey in
winter with my stay-at-home habits.

"On one condition, however, I might. If when
you take that oath of conformity to the doctrine, discipline, etc., of the Protestant Episcopal Church, which
in a narrow, sectistic spirit is made the *first* act in the
consecration office (your consecrators will have nothing to do with you until after you have sworn to be
an out-and-out Episcopalian : you may be sound in
the Catholic faith and in all evangelical doctrine ;
you may be qualified for your apostolical functions, but
you shall not exercise them, you shall be no apostle,
until you obligate yourself, in the most solemn language that can be uttered, that you will adhere to a
certain ritual and discipline, for the most part confessedly of human origin and authority. If such a

[1] *Evangelical Catholic Papers*, pp. 181–184.

promise be necessary, it might be made with some grace *after* all the others, as an accidental, not an essential, or at least secondary, not a primary, requirement. It is a most extraordinary opening of an inauguration of a Peter, Paul, or John; so little and contracted, compared with what follows in that truly apostolical office !).

"To return to what I began to say: if, when you take the Protestant Episcopal Church oath, you will make an audible reservation in words to this effect: 'So long as I shall believe that there is nothing in the same hindering my liberty and duty as a bishop in the Universal Church of Christ,' I should certainly make an effort to come and witness such an advance towards Catholic liberty in the episcopate.

"You would then be open to liberal arguments and considerations against which you will feel yourself canon-bound. Of course you will do no such thing. You mean to be a Protestant Episcopal Church bishop, — nothing more. You mean to be the ecclesiastic of the peculiar type which you now are : you will make no proviso for any possible future enlightenment; you will fancy yourself a Catholic bishop while you ignore hundreds of ministers around you sound in the Catholic faith, and true preachers of the Lord Jesus Christ. You will treat them as bearing no commission (although they show every sign of one from the Holy Ghost) : yet, should they ask communion at your hands, you will refuse it, unless they bow, like you, to a compliance with institutions and practices not pretended to be divine.

"You will grant authority to preach the everlasting gospel only on very peculiar ecclesiastical conditions. . . . For that I am sorry; yet I am thankful for your promotion. I believe, as I said in my last, that you will be a good shepherd of the flock committed to your care. I think you will be the most gospel bishop of all your High Church brethren in the House. I will trust your heart to get the better of your logic. I will fain hope, at least pray, that your episcopate will be a centre of unity in Western Pennsylvania, — not that *barrier* to unity which most of our bishops now are. Write yourself when you really *are* Bishop of Pittsburgh." [1]

Twenty-five years ago, the sentiments contained in this most remarkable letter were looked upon as an old man's harmless dream. To-day the American church is on its knees before God asking Him to guide it, so that it may strive to realize this veritable catholicity, in the presence of that spurious growth of so-called Catholic sentiment which is at the best but the fungous accretion of a cavernous antiquity. The following extracts will sufficiently indicate his positions with regard to the order and freedom of worship: —

"A church without a liturgy hardly seems a church at all; it lacks the great means of social worship which has been employed in all ages, and which, indeed, seems essential to church life, not to say what a safeguard of the truth it throws away. It has

[1] *Life of Bishop Kerfoot*, vol. ii. pp. 417, 418.

gone to a dangerous extreme. But is there not an
opposite extreme, — not equally dangerous, indeed,
but still an extreme? And is it not that to which we
Episcopalians are addicted, — the utter proscription of
all free prayer? The union of the two methods is by
no means impracticable. It existed in the churches
on the continent for some two centuries after the
Reformation, and still continues in those which adhere
to the Augsburg Confession.[1] That possibly we are
at an extreme in the matter, might be suspected from
the fact that we are more bound up by ritual prescription than any other church in Christendom is, or
ever was.[2]

"In the Church of Rome, uniformity is prescribed
in the offices of the mass and the sacraments, and
to some extent, for matins and vespers; after which
there is no end to the diversity of her services, nor
need they be in any two places alike. It is her study
to engage the people by all manner of devotions,
rites, and ceremonies, for which the license allowed
her clergy is quite an opposite to the limit imposed
on ours. Indeed, our peculiarity in not recognizing
anything as profitable in public devotion but what is
set down for us *verbatim et literatim*, is without a
parallel in the history of our religion. This might
suggest the misgiving whether it be a wise peculiarity.
In fact, if we have not got to the extreme, where is

[1] To proscribe liturgies, as nearly all the Protestants of this
country have done, is to be *uncatholic;* to proscribe all freedom in prayer is to be unevangelical.

[2] *Evangelical Catholic Papers*, First Series, pp. 132, 133.

it ? How could we be tied up any tighter than we are ? Still, if we like it, and don't see that it is an extreme, if it is not too tight for us, very well, but let us not insist on forcing it upon everybody else. In performing said service, ' NO OTHER prayers shall be used than those prescribed in said book.' [1] No, not after the sermon any more than before it. This an honest construction of the canon obliges us to admit. No prayer out of book, whether from the desk or the pulpit, — no free outpouring of the preacher's heart for God's blessing on his words. He has been calling sinners to repentance, warning them to flee from the wrath to come ; or he has been pointing believers to their heavenly inheritance, entreating them, by all the glories before them, to press onwards to the prize. His soul, all aglow, glows on into ardent groanings for the Spirit to descend and inflame the hearers' hearts. ' Dear brethren, let us pray,' he would ear-nestly invite them, but he dares not, unless perchance he finds a collect, or patches one or two together to eke out some allusion to his subject. ' Pray on,' says the spirit struggling within him ; ' Be quiet,' says the law. In the cold look of some high and dry hearer he sees the canon pointed at him, and down he sits, loyally smothering the divine but uncanonical im-pulse, — a dutiful son of the church. Of what church, my dear bishop ? Of the church that sings her *Veni Creator?* Of the church that asks for her prophets the tongues of fire ? Bondage all this ! Pardon me if bondage I call it, unworthy of the liberty where-

[1] From the 45th Canon, 1832.

with Christ hath made us free. Men feel it to be bondage. They will not endure it.[1] The highest authority which the church can plead for ritual enactments is the divine prescription of the Lord's Prayer. But let not the sanction of that prescription be pushed too far. Our Lord gave one set form. He did not forbid all other forms. Rather, while He enjoined a literal use of that (so let it be assumed), He designed it to be the model of other prayers. 'Thus pray ye,' — not only in these words, but let them be the sum and substance of all your prayers. So the Church has understood her Lord. She enjoins his prayer *verbatim* in each of her offices, and adds further prayers in accordance with it. The whole liturgy may be regarded as a development of the Lord's Prayer. To say this, is its highest eulogy. But let not the Church claim more for her development than her Lord has done for his original. As He did not say in these words and these alone ye shall pray, so let not her make that exclusive demand for the forms which she has wrought out from those words.

"Let her not claim for her half-inspired compositions more than is claimed by its Author for the composition wholly inspired. As if the liturgy had exhausted the Lord's Prayer, let her not proceed to put a seal on our lips in a syllable beyond. Let her liturgy answer the double purpose of the Lord's Prayer, — a set form and a directory of devotion. The canon forbids its use as a directory, and so far diminishes its practical value. This is not to follow

---

[1] *Evangelical Catholic Papers*, First Series, pp. 213, 214.

the example of the Master, — it is to exceed it. Unlike Him, his church — no! the canon, which is an excrescence on the church — says, Thus and thus only shall ye pray. Cut off the excrescence. Let the church be content to exercise no more exclusive prerogative than her Master; and from Him let her learn to teach her members, especially her ministers, as He taught his disciples.[1]

.   .   .   .

"That which the liturgy is not — cannot from its very nature be — is the expression of wants and feelings peculiar to an individual member, or to a certain number of individual members, of the church. Our liturgy has no utterance for what they would utter as individuals. It knows nothing of their particular wants or experience. But then shall these never have leave to vent themselves in the sanctuary? Shall these be denied an utterance? Shall private griefs and joys be kept in abeyance, and be commanded to be still, in the house of prayer and praise? In the communion office, which is eminently THE liturgy, shall not the absent, the sick, the dying communicant be permitted to send in his petitions to his pastor and brethren, to be offered by them amid the sacred mysteries, when intercessions, we may believe, are most availing? The liturgy does not forbid that. It is not so cold-hearted. It would pause, so to speak, in its general offices, to give opportunity to the single supplicant. It stops for the preacher to go into his sermon; and when prayer is connected with

[1] *Evangelical Catholic Papers*, pp. 314, 315.

it, why should it not also stop for him as a merciful and compassionate priest, — pleading with God in such words as he can, and as best suit the case, for the poor brother or sister who begs to be remembered as present in spirit at the sacred feast? Let the liturgy be considered as the common voice of the whole church, and special prayers as the voice of particular congregations; we shall then hear no more of our dishonoring the former by asking free liberty in the latter.[1]

"The non-enactment of any canons touching the laity equivalent to those in England, by our American church, is significant, and may be understood as designed to leave the evangelical liberties of laymen untouched. The 'conventicles' unlawful in the English Church are not unlawful in ours. Laymen may not 'prophesy' there; they may here. Usage, indeed, is against it, and usage may be considered part of the system of the church, but that will not be so when the church comes to understand and develop more fully her office as the prophet of the Lord.[2] We ask no option in the use of the Prayer Book, that is, in the regular congregations of the church, to which alone we would have some authoritative declaration that the conjunction is confined, leaving missionaries and others circumstanced like them to pray as they can.

"It is not the PREscription but the PROscription of the canon at which we demur. We are not 'weary

[1] *Evangelical Catholic Papers*, pp. 316, 317.
[2] *Ibid.*, pp. 228, 229.

of the liturgy,' but we are weary, quite weary, of
the restraint of a law which fastens a bondage to the
liturgy in no wise belonging to it; which has no authority in Holy Writ, no precedent in early Christian
practice, and no parallel in any branch of the church
at the present day; which abridges evangelical liberty, and is an anomaly in Catholic legislation; which
suffers not the pastor of his flock to pray as he will
with his flock in the very midst of his own fold; which
denies him, as the father of his spiritual family, the
privilege, enjoyed by every other father, of freely
mingling his heart with theirs at the altar of their
sanctuary home; which sets bounds to the congregation as well, in their approaches to God, seeing that
as a congregation they can approach Him only through
their minister, — if their spokesman be restrained, so
are they; which thus disfranchises the citizens of the
Heavenly City touching their right of petition, dic-
tating the words in which alone it shall be exercised,
and that in the public assemblies of the citizens in
which petition is the most availing; which infringes
the Magna Charta of freedom in prayer guaranteed
by the great Apostle of gospel liberty when he bids
us come, whether in closet or church, to the throne
of grace boldly, literally with freespokenness; which
makes the church conflict not only with an Apostle,
but transcend the sanction of her Lord in ordaining
prayer by set form, seeing that while He prescribed
one form He did not, by common consent, forbid all
other forms; which dares to outlaw the very prayers
of Holy Writ, except so far as they are adopted in

the Prayer Book; which is an interdict so monstrous
(as it seems to us) that nothing can be said for it but
that it is a protection against prayers in bad taste, as
if chaste rhetoric were an essential quality of acceptable devotion, and our clergy, with all their ritual
training, could not be trusted to make a becoming
prayer! Ay, of this we are weary, and earnestly do
we pray for relief. We beg only for ourselves;
others, men of prayer and far better than we, may
feel no grievance. The privilege granted us will
be no imposition on them. Those who think with
us may be a minority, for aught we know a small
minority, but minorities deserve consideration, — at
least when they are claiming what they believe to be
their rights. Now, how comes it to pass that some of
our brethren regard our earnestness on this point as
a sign of disaffection to the liturgy, and go so far as
to tell us that we would 'substitute in the place of it
the crude effervescence of extemporary prayer?'
Does it not arise from their misconception, or a for-
getfulness of what the liturgy really is, and of its
proper function in the church? May we venture,
then, to remind men what its nature and purpose
are, and what they are not? The liturgy is the common voice of the whole church, — the solemn oblation
of prayer and praise due everywhere in all her congregations, 'from the rising of the sun even unto the
going down of the same.' As such, the liturgy
changes not; the Great Being to whom its service is
offered, and the church who offers it, changing never.
To make it in any part extemporary would be to

violate its nature. It can consist of no new or raw materials. To be a meet offering, it must be of the choicest products, — the gold, the frankincense, and the myrrh, the 'compound of sweet spices' gathered and selected by the church from all her storehouses of devotion; and such, if such be anywhere in Christendom, is our liturgy, — especially that which is the liturgy proper, the communion office. This, then, is its true idea; the Catholic service of the Catholic Church, or of any branch thereof. Accordingly, it is not the peculiar voice of any one congregation, much less of any member of a congregation. Its confessions, adorations, and thanksgivings are common to the whole body of the faithful. Whatever does not belong to the whole body, and cannot be uttered by all the faithful, is foreign to the liturgy. Hence the special prayers of a particular congregation do not belong to it. In the far greater part, indeed, the prayers of any congregation will be identical with the Common Prayer of the church, and in that find all the expression they need. But the two are not always identical. Every congregation, either from temporary circumstances or from fellow-feeling with some of its members, has its own subjects of supplication and praise for which the Common Prayer does not supply the adequate expression. It is not designed to supply it; such is not its office: its office is general, not particular. Its utterances are those of the whole body, not of the separate parts; but — and *here is the question* — shall the separate parts, say the congregations, have no utterances of their own? Is it the province of

the liturgy to hold them dumb in aught pertaining immediately to themselves? Is it her prerogative to monopolize the sanctuary, and to hush therein the lisping of a syllable beyond her own? Has not each assembly of God's elect its own JUBILATES, and MISE-RERES, and outpouring of its own griefs and joys, or the griefs and joys of its members, which it adopts as its own? While, as a *liturgus*, I celebrate the liturgy, and do all my duty in that regard, may I never, as an *evangelist*, pray as I am moved for the conversion of the sinners to whom I preach? or, as an under - shepherd of the sheep committed to my care, am I never to plead in their behalf and among them, without restraint, to the Great Shepherd, who, while He cares for his world-wide flock, has a tender interest in his sheep one by one, — who 'gathers the lambs in his arm, and carries them in his bosom'? Is the genius of the liturgy so cold-hearted? No, it is not the genius of the liturgy. It is not the spirit of the church, of whose charity the liturgy is full. It is an extraordinary act of legislation, which, how-ever it found its way into the statute book, if allowed to continue there, can only be with the understand-ing that it is not to be enforced. Let not, then, things which are distinct in their nature and purpose be confounded. The Liturgy, the Common Prayer, is one thing, — free prayer, special prayer (in words original or selected, written or extemporary), is an-other. Each has its own sphere, — neither interferes with the other. We may contend with equal ear-nestness for both. To one I am bound as a presbyter of the church; the other I claim as a minister of Christ's gospel, standing 'fast in the liberty wherewith He has made us free.' Only let this distinction be understood and acted on. Those who now seem to differ so widely will then be glad to bear with one another as brethren, and, while adhering to their own preferences, will be happy in coming to a brotherly agreement." [1]

II.

The unique feature of Dr. Muhlenberg's churchmanship was that there were no self-delusions in it. He started with no *à priori* assumptions. Unlike Newman, he did not begin with the arbitrary postulate that there must be a visible Holy Catholic Church somewhere, and then proceed to reason that the Anglican Communion is not it, as it has not the distinguishing notes of Catholicity, and that therefore the Church of Rome must be it. On the contrary, he addressed himself to the inquiry whether there were any Holy Catholic Church visible anywhere in this world; and that inquiry compelled him soberly to conclude and manfully acknowledge that no such Catholic institution existed, nor had existed on the earth, since that dark day so many centuries ago, when the Pope of Rome anathematized and excommunicated the Greek patriarchs and the Eastern Church.

[1] *Evangelical Catholic Papers*, pp. 293–298.

The Roman Church, with its twofold yoke of assent to the Tridentine Creed and loyalty to the papal autocracy as the twin tests of Catholicity, he regarded as perhaps the farthest from Apostolic Catholicity of any church in Christendom.

Turning to the different denominations of Protestant Christianity, he found that they made no claim to Catholicity, and even manifested a sort of prejudice against the word itself as savoring too much of Romanist pretension and arrogance. They were Catholic neither in creed nor practice, nor was this their aim. Anglican Catholicity he found, upon the most patient and prolonged investigation, to be no less a figment and no less an *ism* than Roman Catholicism. He was broader and more searching in his analysis than Newman, if less erudite, and equally unflinching in his verdict. In the thoroughgoing Erastianism of the mother church, irrespective of any other feature, he recognized, with the glance of common sense, an effectual bar to catholicity. The American branch of the Anglo-Catholic communion — the Protestant Episcopal Church in the United States of America — he knew to be toiling in the bondage of sect. Her worship was non-catholic in point of PROscription ; her system was sectarian in point of PREscription. She made stalwart claims

to historic catholicity, but this was not the style
of catholicity which Dr. Muhlenberg held aloft
as his ideal. If the historic catholicity were not
likewise a living and actual catholicity, he knew
that it could bring no helpful force or message
to the present age; and unfortunately the living
and actual catholicity of the Protestant Episcopal Church, in her semi-colonial narrowness, was
discredited and positively disproven by present
and indisputable facts of her practice.

Dr. Muhlenberg made no moan over this dis-
covery. The sorrow which this vision of the
real state of the Christian world entailed upon
the soul of the seer remained locked in the pri-
vacy of his own breast. He never agonized in
public; he was incapable of writing such a subtle piece of subjective analysis as an *Apologia
pro vita sua.* Having recognized the unwelcome
facts of the situation, he proclaimed them, and
while doing so employed himself in the most
natural and matter-of-fact methods available for
the accomplishment of some effective remedy.
As the great prophets of the Old Testament
were preëminently men of action and efficiency
in practical affairs, so was it with this gospel
and church prophet of our time. His efforts
for the practical reformation of modern Christianity, in its church aspects, extended in two
different directions, and were exercised in two

separate spheres, viz., in the parish of the Holy Communion, and in the Protestant Episcopal Church at large. He boldly struck, in his own words, for "emancipating the episcopate," and "unsectarizing the church." [1] The history and results of his work in this latter direction form the subject of the succeeding chapter.

III.

In his own parochial ministrations Dr. Muhlenberg boldly exercised a large part of that catholic and evangelical liberty for which he so earnestly contended in behalf of his brethren of the clergy, and of the laity as well, in the church at large. The broad principles of churchmanship, enunciated in the foregoing excerpts from his published papers, found their practical application and their embodied working in the church and parish of the Holy Communion during his rectorship there. The chief purpose of this enterprise was the establishment of a free church, where the rich and the poor might meet together in the house of the Lord. One of the leading motives that prompted him to initiate the "Memorial Movement" was the hope of attaining some authorized modification of the church system and worship which would enable her to deal more effectively with the masses of the peo-

[1] These two expressions are Dr. Muhlenberg's own creation.

ple. He found it everywhere an acknowledged
fact, that the Protestant Episcopal Church was
the church of the rich, and not of the common
people, and one of his leading aims was to remedy this defect by securing greater flexibility
and adaptation of church methods to popular
needs. The result of his example is most marked
to-day in the church life of the metropolis, with
its free and cosmopolitan type of churchmanship. In the case of his own parish, he brought
this problem to a satisfactory solution, and
afforded a living illustration of many of the
changes in method which he advocated. As a
concrete example is much more attractive than
any statement of abstract principles, it will be
interesting before the close of this chapter to
review the salient features of Dr. Muhlenberg's
work in this parish and their main results. The
church, as has been said, was free, being supported wholly by the offertory. Whether there
was any understanding with reference to the
customary occupancy of particular pews by the
different families composing the parish, we are
not informed. In the matter of voluntary offerings, however, the people were taught to give according to their several ability. At first there
was an understanding between the more wealthy
members as to the approximate sums necessary
for each to contribute in order to meet the aggre-

gate expenses; but with the further growth of the parish, and the establishment of the people in the principles and the habit of giving, this became unnecessary and was discontinued. A very large proportion of the poorer class of people soon became attached to the church, and were counted among its regular worshipers, many of them also being communicants. Through the example, the teaching, and the influence of Dr. Muhlenberg, the wealthier members of the flock came more and more into a very tender and real sympathy with these humbler ones. The atmosphere of the church in its worship and in its social life was that of a true household of God. The Fatherhood of Him from whom every fatherhood in heaven and earth is named was a realized fact in the knowledge and experience of the individual; and the consequent brotherhood of men became a living reality in the common life.

It was the writer's privilege some years ago to travel in Italy with Dr. Muhlenberg's successor at the Church of the Holy Communion, Rev. F. E. Lawrence, D. D., and to learn from him, as well as from the present zealous and self-denying rector of the same church, Rev. Henry Mottet, D. D., many incidents which show the founder of this church in a new, and strong, and unfamiliar light.

It is doubtless true that too many stories and gossipy anecdotes tend to cheapen the character of our ideal saints and heroes. Strong characters need the shadow element as truly as they need the element of light; and the electric glare of too great familiarity tends to do away with that healthful obscurity which is necessary to conserve and recruit the world's great personalities.

A man should always be a hero to his biographer, — if he fails to be a hero to his valet, — and one of the strongest and most potent elements in all hero-worship is the strongly recognized element of reserve.

Passing over these minor incidents of parochial life, we find that the same line of practical endeavor followed the vast development of charitable and benevolent organization, which unquestionably took its departure from the point of his influence and personality. Church organization of charity there was little previous to Dr. Muhlenberg. In this, as in so many other directions of practical Christian achievement, he was a pioneer. Even in parish organization for practical work he was creative. Not to speak in this connection of the first Protestant Sisterhood in America, established by him as a parish auxiliary in the Church of the Holy Communion, he originated an employment society for furnishing needle-work to the indigent women of the parish, a Church Dispensary under the care of the Sisterhood, and the Fresh-air Fund. This latter phrase, and the thing corresponding, were both original with him. Besides these original and distinctive enterprises in parish organization, there were, a day school for boys, and another for girls, Thanksgiving feasts and the church Christmas trees for the poor. Parish organization for benevolent work was, indeed, about as backward in the metropolis as was corporate charity, until Dr. Muhlenberg gave it the impulsion of his creative and powerful genius. But it was the innovations in the customary order of worship which he practiced in the Church of the Holy Communion, which subjected him to the largest share of suspicion and misunderstanding. He made no pretensions, of course, to the liturgical license which he fearlessly practiced in the private chapel of the institute at Flushing, and at St. Paul's College; but a man of Dr. Muhlenberg's spiritual genius and poetic instincts could not be placed in church relations that did not admit of the exercise of a legitimate freedom. To begin, he took a decided departure from established customs in this land by establishing a daily service. Almost if not the first daily service of public worship ever maintained in this country was instituted by Dr. Muh-

lenberg in the Church of the Holy Communion. With regard to this service he thus expressed himself in the " Evangelical Catholic,"
1851 : —

" If there were no other argument for the constant
morning and evening prayer in our churches (and we
confess that its expediency in all cases is a question),
there is one which should weigh with Protestants, viz.,
that the Holy Scriptures are thus publicly read, in
course, for the benefit of all who choose to hear.
This is a great office for which our church has provided, and which we believe is peculiar to her among
the churches in Christendom. She is thus a perpetual preacher of the pure word of God. Though
there be but a solitary few to listen, she acquits herself of her duty in proclaiming the whole counsel of
her Lord. The thought is indeed sublime, that from
year to year, from age to age, her voice as God's
prophet keeps sounding on, in the same old words of
Holy Writ, ceaseless and constant in its utterance as
the rising and setting of the sun."

How far he was from being blind to the
possible abuses and mischiefs of such a service
is evident from the following letter to Doctor
Kerfoot : —

" *May* 2, 1848.

" My advice with regard to the daily service I must
give you in a few words. If you introduce it, by no
means make attendance compulsory on the boys, not

even on the communicants. A short service morning and evening is enough for any of them. I tell my own people that I do not wish to see them twice a day at church, except those who have leisure thus to consecrate.

" Family and private devotions I know are suffering from this fashion (for I fear it is getting to be such) for church-going. Besides, ' Dearly Beloved ' twice a day is an absurd formality, both for minister and people; and the confession and absolution so constantly repeated is unfavorable to genuine penitence, and any due appreciation of the ' pardoning power of the priest.' Whatever it be, all our services of course must be penitential, more or less, and the frequent use of ' Kyrie Eleison ' in all liturgies is very proper. But that is very different from a solemn and regular confession and absolution at every morning and evening prayers. You know it was not so in the first book, and it was not until after several reviews that these additions were made to the evening prayer. If I had time I would write a tract on this subject that would convince *everybody* that I am right. Be mainly concerned about your boys ' entering into their closets,' and their using themselves to ejaculatory prayer wherever they are. Nevertheless, wherever practicable, I think that a parish church should be open morning and evening, that the people may repair thither whenever they can, and find the priest ministering there in behalf of the whole congregation. So great is my dread of frequent and long public services upon children, that it is my chief objection to choristers chanting the service daily. Look at the English Cathedral boys. I inquired of the organist of Westminster whether some of them did not become clergymen. He never heard of such a thing ! "

In a letter to his dear friend Dr. Kerfoot he writes as follows : [1] —

"*November* 26, 1852.

" There is something more than a fancy in Evangelical Catholicism. For example, the sacraments, — the Catholic regards them as God coming to us in them, and hence cannot say too much of their efficacy : he considers them objectively. The Evangelical thinks only of his coming to God in the sacraments, and hence is taken up with his own faith and dispositions in order to their efficacy : he considers them subjectively. The Roman Catholic, and the Anglo-Catholic too, is intensely *objective* in his view of the sacraments. The Evangelical, or rather the " E "vangelical, is intensely subjective : the Evangelical Catholic considers them both objectively and subjectively, and hence is right. So of faith, — the Catholic asks *what* he is to believe, the Evangelical *how* he is to believe. . . . All through, Catholicism is objective, as you will see on trial. . . . Catholicism, unchecked, leads to consolidated churchism and superstition ; Evangelicalism, to individualism and rationalism."

Dr. Muhlenberg was also among the first to inaugurate the practice of a weekly celebration

[1] *Life of Kerfoot*, by Hall Harrison, pp. 130, 131.

of the holy communion. This step was not taken, however, until after he had been for some time rector of the Church of the Holy Communion, and knew something of the temper and needs of his people. There was nothing whatever of the Mass idea in his underlying motive for this innovation. Nor was it with the idea of encouraging frequent receptions of the sacrament that he established such a usage.

No one appreciated more nearly at their true value than he, the possible dangers of such a custom, remembering the innate tendency to superstition in the human mind; and later in life he seemed more clearly to recognize the importance of enlarging more frequently upon these dangers. Nevertheless he deemed it a matter of very considerable moment, in a church like that of the Holy Communion, that all should have full and free opportunity to partake with something like regularity. The weekly celebration he regarded as extremely valuable in offering the comforts and helps of the sacrament to those who, on account of some personal experience of grief or joy, most needed it, and at the time when they most needed it.

The people were clearly taught that each communicant was not expected to partake each Lord's day; but the holy table was spread each recurring Lord's day, in order that all might have equal and abundant opportunity to partake. Intimately associated with this custom, and almost necessitated by the reason which led to its establishment, was the division of the offices in the Sunday service, which he was the first to introduce. Instead of following the traditional practice of one continuous service for morning prayer, litany, and holy communion, he took a step in the direction of return to the ancient custom of employing these distinct offices at separate times.

The regular order for morning prayer was observed at nine o'clock; followed by the litany, ante-communion service, sermon, and offertory at half-past ten. Then, dispersing for an interval of some fifteen minutes, the congregation reassembled at twelve for the holy communion.

This made it possible for all the members of the different households in the parish to be present at one at least of the Sunday services, and also to receive the holy communion certainly as often as once a month, or oftener if desired. In many of these services conducted by Dr. Muhlenberg at the Church of the Holy Communion, it is evident that the pattern which he had before his mind was that of St. Peter's, Philadelphia, with which he had been familiar in his early days. These, however, were not the only novel features introduced by Dr. Muhlenberg into the worship of the Church of the Holy Communion. The fact that forty years ago the chanting of the psalter antiphonally by the choir in the church was among the many innovations which caused no little stir among the dry bones of a stereotyped and formal conservatism, may appear surprising to the churchman of to-day.

He also had the temerity to join the few who were discarding the black gown of the period for the use of the surplice in preaching. He did this because he felt that the gown had become the badge of a party, while the surplice was the standard uniform of every minister of the church.

We of to-day can with difficulty imagine a time when Christmas-trees were not; yet when Dr. Muhlenberg introduced the custom of a parish Christmas-tree, it was almost an unheard-of experiment, as were also the matins of Christmas and Easter which he instituted.

He gave to the celebration of the Epiphany something of its true character as a missionary festival, by devoting to the cause of missions the very large offerings which he taught his people to give at that season. These things, in addition to the charitable organizations of the parish, — such as the employment society for helping the poor women of the church, the Sisterhood, the church dispensary, church infirmary, and church schools, — were original contributions of Dr. Muhlenberg's personality to what we recognize as the customary and commonplace churchmanship of to-day.

In the administration of his own parish, he found place and opportunity for the exercise of that evangelical freedom and liturgic license in special occasions of church worship, for which he so earnestly contended in public during the succeeding years of his life. He furnished an instance of this on the occasion of a young clergyman's departure as a missionary to Wisconsin, where, from having been a pupil of Dr. Muhlenberg's, he was called to minister to a colony from the Church of the Holy Communion, which bore the same name as the mother church. On Sunday, September 16th, his fifty-third birthday, in addition to the regular morning and afternoon services, he held in the church a sort of missionary meeting, beginning with the Lord's Prayer as they knelt, followed by the versicles. The choir sang an anthem and the " Benedic ; " there was a lesson from Isaiah, thirty-fifth chapter, and some remarks from the rector, introducing Bishop Kemper, of Wisconsin, who gave an interesting address with reference to the work in his diocese, and a happy allusion to the colony, the Church of the Holy Communion, to whom the mother church of the same name was about to send a minister. Then followed a few parting words to the missionary from the rector, a missionary hymn, a few collects, including the one in the institution office, and the benediction by the bishop. The service was hearty, and very effective in kindling a missionary enthusiasm among the people, many of whom remained to bid the missionary good-by after the services; but a couple of church dignitaries, and a number of city clergy who were present, held aloof with such evident coldness and disapproval of the irregularity in the service as to provoke the doctor's exclamation, " Can we do nothing except we begin, ' Dearly beloved brethren ' ? Are rubrics to be the choke-strings of the heart ? "

Dr. Muhlenberg, in the Church of the Holy Communion, also organized the first boy choir ever successfully employed in New York in connection with the service of praise. He had an unqualified abhorrence of the regulation quartette choir, and his musical accomplishments and fine taste enabled him to develop this element of the service, by means of congregational singing led by the choir of boys, to an exceptional degree of beauty and perfection.

It is difficult at the present period, when most of these practices have become customary throughout the entire church, to realize the comment which they elicited at the time. His heroic, and apparently in its calmness, uncon-

scious, departure from the stereotyped formality
and coldness of the worship at that time, subjected him to all manner of suspicions, and even
opprobrium, which he silently bore, knowing
how unjust and unfounded they were. When
the hour came, however, for achieving a higher
purpose than mere self-vindication, he boldly
undeceived his false accusers in a manner that
created much more excitement, and subjected
him to a larger share of uncharitable judgment
in the opposite direction than his supposed
ritualistic or Romanizing tendencies had done.
But the history of this belongs to the Memorial
Movement and the following chapter.

All the unwarrantable inferences of his suspicious critics with regard to his ritual beliefs
were drawn, as he himself said, "from what
they thought they saw, never from what they
heard." It came from the old sin of putting
a prosaic interpretation or construction upon
things in their nature poetical. The influence of
Dr. Muhlenberg's example, however, in his personal ministrations in the Church of the Holy
Communion was as potent towards the realization of that Evangelical and Catholic liberty
toward which the church is now so steadily advancing, as was his public championship of the
cause in the Memorial Movement, — perhaps
more powerful, because more silent, subtle, and
irresistible in its secret operation.

THE HISTORY OF THE MEMORIAL MOVEMENT.

"As we review the history of the ecclesiastical reaction which now shows signs of having spent its force, it is safe to say that the crusade against the human reason, in which Newman was a leading representative, has not been successful. What the age now demands is the enforcement of the principles for which the reason has been furnishing the materials in superabundant measure. The effort to repress the reason has come too late in the world's history to attain success. The tide of things is setting more and more strongly against ecclesiastical obscuration. We owe another debt to Newman and to Mansel than those we generally acknowledge. The one has shown in a typical way, which has had no such illustration since the days of Augustine, how distrust of the reason must logically end in acknowledging an infallible pope. The other, in his chivalric attempt to defend the traditional dogmas, or to overcome the Germanism, as he called it, which was infecting the church, could accomplish his purpose only by cutting away the foundations on which the possibility of a revelation rests.

"These instances teach us anew that modern Christianity is committed to progress and growth in the knowledge of God and of his revelation.

"If it is dangerous to advance it is only more dangerous to retreat. The human reason at last is free, and is increasingly realizing what freedom means. Christianity must now trust, as indeed it is trusting, to its own merits for its vindication to the reason. It must stand or fall, as it can show itself to be true." — REV. A. V. G. ALLEN, *Continuity of Christian Thought*.

"Is it, then, to be the end of all our litigations, theories, and attempted scientific constructions, that after our heats of controversy have cooled, and our fires of extirpation have quite burned away, we come back to the same kind of preaching alphabet in which the first fathers had their simple beginnings? Be it so. And yet the labor we have spent has been by no means lost: we shall come back into that preaching with an immense advantage gained over those fathers. What they did in their simplicity, we shall do in a way of well-directed reason. Their simplicity, in fact, supposed the certainty of all these long detours of labor and contest to come afterwards; but we, in our return, come back with our experiments all made and detours all ended, not simply to preach Christ just in their manner, but to do it because we have finally proved the wisdom of it, and the foolishness of everything else, — advantages which are worth to us all they have cost." — BUSHNELL.

CHAPTER IV.

In the fall of the year 1853, as a boy of ten years of age, I remember going to the General Convention of the Episcopal Church held in St. John's Church, in New York.

A great movement of some sort was on hand, and I remember distinctly the impression created upon my mind when a delegation of clergymen, headed by a striking looking man with a poetic face, walked up the main aisle, and presented a written document to the dignified presiding officer of the House of Clerical and Lay Deputies, the Rev. Dr. Creighton of Tarrytown, New York. It was Dr. Muhlenberg who headed the procession on that occasion; the Memorial Papers formed the document then presented; and the little boy in the pew was the unconscious historian who, in the present chapter, seeks to describe this historic event in the history of the Episcopal Church in the United States of America. Strangely enough, for years afterwards, whenever the thought of the poet Dante was presented to my mind, it always seemed as if somewhere, either here or in some preëxistent life, I had once seen the man who has pictured for us "The Inferno," "The Purgatorio," and "The Paradiso," and was in some strange way familiar with his face. This confused impression never was explained until one day, when looking at a photograph of Dr. Muhlenberg, it flashed upon my mind that I had confounded the two appearances, and that the face, seen as a child in the far-off convention, had come to stand as the face of the poet Dante.

The recently published life of Dr. Muhlenberg, together with his "Memorial Papers," have made this position which he took upon the subject of church expansion familiar to all students of present church history. There is nothing in the history of the American Church so fraught with great possibilities as the outline of the future which he sketched with a firm hand and a believing soul. This vision is for an appointed time; and the seer, being dead, yet speaketh. The lesser objects sought for in these Memorial Papers, such as the relaxation of the stereotype order of services and the enrichment and flexibility of the liturgy, have been already attained. The one great object of his life, as he pressed again and again for the appointment, by the General Convention, of a standing Episcopal commission upon the subject of church unity, yet awaits accomplishment. The day for its realization has been postponed until two results have been gained by the church at large : first, its deeper sense of the need of a unification of Protestant Christendom, as new and unforeseen dangers thicken upon us; and, secondly, a faith that will accept this high ideal as among the possibilities, according to our Lord's words, — " All things are possible to him that believeth."

The principal object of the Memorial was to liberalize and utilize the latent and hitherto inoperative forces of the church. This Memorial Movement looked both to the liberalizing of the Episcopal Church within the bounds of lawful freedom, and also to the practical precedent which it set to the Christians of other names in the scattered ranks of Protestantism. Dr. Muhlenberg explained its twofold object in the series of papers which he called the " Evangelical Catholic Papers."

Much of the information upon this subject, as well as the motive-power which first lodged the Muhlenberg conception of Catholic Christianity in the writer's mind, came from the inspiration of one of the most precious friendships of younger days in the ministry, the strong and fraternal friendship of that large-hearted father of yesterday, Dr. Edward A. Washburn, who, with his helpful and sympathetic wife in the spacious study of Calvary rectory in New York, always made it a privilege to listen to the stories of this true saint of God.

This friend, whose body now rests by the side of his saintly companion in the quiet shades of the realized dream of St. Johnland, thus speaks of him : —

"It was then (at the date of the Memorial) that I first knew him personally ; and never can I forget the impression he left on me. He was at his ripest age. The glow of youth had passed into a large wisdom, but there was childlike faith, — the intuition of the heart, the broken torrent of eloquent speech, the grand, catholic aspiration. Every conversation on the Memorial comes back to me. It was his conviction that our church needed to act, with all its capabilities, in the vast, growing field of missions and of ministries for all conditions of men. But more than this, he felt that the best way of reconciliation for our strifes was larger room for real work. High and low parties were wasting their strength in quarrel over rubrics. The strife, in his view, was embittered because both were hemmed within the small area of an inflexible system. At this very hour a large part of the freedom which the Memorial asked is virtually gained." [1]

The immediate aim of the Memorial Move-

[1] *Vine out of Egypt*, p. 110.

ment was to secure larger practical results in popular evangelization and religious training.

It was undertaken in consequence of Dr. Muhlenberg's painful conviction — as he viewed the widespread and acknowledged alienation of the masses from her — that the Church was not fulfilling her commission as a missionary organization. It was the practical exigency, and the effort to provide a practical remedy for existing evils, that determined his action. The great ulterior result contemplated as incidental to this noble design was, however, nothing less ideal than the restoration of a genuine Catholic unity from the isolated fragments of a dismembered Protestantism. Thus the ideal and the actual, the poetic and the practical, were ever wedded in the vision of this poet-workman.

As the nearest means of entering upon the march toward the realization of these grand aims, the Memorialists, as we have seen, boldly struck for " emancipating the episcopate," to use Dr. Muhlenberg's expressive words, " and unsectarizing the church." The first point to be gained, in Dr. Muhlenberg's estimation, was an ecclesiastical system, broader and more comprehensive, and at the same time more flexible, than was at that time administered in the Protestant Episcopal Church. The manner of inaugurating the Movement was characteristic, and illustrated

Dr. Muhlenberg's genius for leadership. That he was born to be a leader of men was manifest in everything that he did. In replying to a friend desiring instruction upon the initiation of a work of charity, and the best methods to be pursued, he strongly advised against beginning with any formal announcement of the work, and against calling together all friends of the movement. Such a course would bring forth a multitude of sterile counsels from the omniscience of friends who affect to know all about the matter, and think their own methods the only right ones. The beginnings of a movement should be always simple and natural, an outgrowth of its own vitality, and nurtured only by those who enter through sympathy and knowledge into its true aims and into the methods of the mind which gave it birth.

This was Dr. Muhlenberg's method of leadership in all his undertakings. His first and uniform impulse was to translate a deep and abiding conviction into the sphere of action, and by his own act and example to determine the direction of such activity. And thus the Memorial Movement was initiated. " What do we mean ? " Dr. Muhlenberg asked. " We call ourselves Catholics. What are we doing for the people, for our brothers and sisters who never hear the gospel preached, who will not come near our churches, who claim that the church is only for the rich ? . . . Our position is alike absurd and unchristian." Then, moreover, he became more and more painfully impressed with the isolation of the Protestant Episcopal Church, and he felt that effort should be made to bring the Christians of this land into something like fellowship on the basis of a common historic faith ; and while he was giving much thought and time to the subject, he suddenly, with that impulsive energy which comes like an inspiration to a man of genius, said to a friend, " Let us prepare a memorial upon this to the House of Bishops, and if we can get no one to sign it, we will sign it ourselves and send it in." This is the origin of the Memorial sent to the House of Bishops in October, 1853, and which is known, and will continue to be known, as the Memorial Movement.[1]

The original document was submitted in the following terms : —

THE MEMORIAL.

To the Bishops of the Protestant Episcopal Church in Council assembled :

" RIGHT REVEREND FATHERS, — The undersigned,

[1] Rev. Dr. Edwin Harwood, from an address before an association of clergymen of which Dr. Muhlenberg was, at the time of his death, the senior member.

presbyters of the church of which you have the over-sight, venture to approach your venerable body with an expression of sentiment which their estimate of your office in relation to the times does not permit them to withhold. In so doing, they have confidence in your readiness to appreciate their motives and their aims. The actual posture of our church, with reference to the great moral and social necessities of the day, presents to the mind of the undersigned a subject of grave and anxious thought. Did they suppose that this was con-fined to themselves, they would not feel warranted in submitting it to your attention ; but they believe it to be participated in by many of their brethren, who may not have seen the expediency of declaring their views, or at least a mature season for such a course.

" The divided and distracted state of our Ameri-can Protestant Christianity, the new and subtle forms of unbelief adapting themselves with fatal success to the spirit of the age, the consolidated forces of Romanism bearing with renewed skill and activity against the Protestant faith, and, as more or less the consequence of these, the utter ignorance of the gos-pel among so large a portion of the lower classes of our population, making a heathen world in our midst, are among the considerations which induce your me-morialists to present the inquiry whether the period has not arrived for the adoption of measures, to meet these exigencies of the times, more comprehensive than any yet provided for by our present ecclesiasti-cal system ; in other words, whether the Protestant

Episcopal Church, with only her present canonical means and appliances, her fixed and invariable modes of public worship, and her traditional customs and usages, is competent to the work of preaching and dispensing the gospel to all sorts and conditions of men, and so adequate to do the work of the Lord in this land and in this age? This question, your petitioners, for their own part, and in consonance with many thoughtful minds among us, believe must be answered in the negative. Their memorial proceeds on the assumption that our church, confined to the exercise of her present system, is not sufficient to the great purposes above mentioned, — that a wider door must be opened for admission to the gospel ministry than that through which her candidates for holy orders are now obliged to enter. Besides such candidates among her own members, it is believed that men can be found among the other bodies of Christians around us who would gladly receive ordination at your hands, could they obtain it without that entire surrender, which would now be required of them, of all the liberty in public worship to which they have been accustomed, — men who could not bring themselves to conform in all particulars to our prescriptions and customs, but yet sound in the faith, and who, having the gifts of preachers and pastors, would be able ministers of the New Testament.

" With deference it is asked, ought such an accession to your means in executing your high commission, ' Go ye into all the world and preach the gospel to every creature,' to be refused, for the sake of conformity in matters recognized in the *Preface to the Book of Common Prayer* as unessentials? Dare we pray the Lord of the harvest to send forth laborers into the harvest while we reject all laborers but those of one peculiar type? The extension of orders to the class of men contemplated (with whatever safeguards, not infringing on evangelical freedom, which your wisdom might deem expedient) appears to your petitioners to be a subject supremely worthy of your deliberations. In addition to the prospect of the immediate good which would thus be opened, an important step would be taken towards the effecting of a church unity in the Protestant Christendom of our land. To become a central bond of union among Christians, who, though differing in name, yet hold to the one faith, the one Lord, and the one baptism, and who need only such a bond to be drawn together in closer and more primitive fellowship, is here believed to be the peculiar province and high privilege of your venerable body as a College of Catholic and Apostolic Bishops *as such.*

" This leads your petitioners to declare the ultimate design of their Memorial, — which is, to submit the practicability, under your auspices, of some ecclesiastical system, broader and more comprehensive than that which you now administer, surrounding and including the Protestant Episcopal Church as it now is, leaving that church untouched, identical with that church in all its great principles, yet providing for as much freedom in opinion, discipline, and worship as is compatible with the essential faith and order of the gospel. To define and act upon such a system, it is believed, must sooner or later be the work of an American Catholic Episcopate.

" In justice to themselves on this occasion, your memorialists beg leave to remark that, although aware that the foregoing views are not confined to their own small number, they have no reason to suppose that any other parties contemplate a public expression of them like the present. Having, therefore, undertaken it, they trust that they have not laid themselves open to the charge of unwarranted intrusion. They find their warrant in the prayer now offered up by all our congregations, ' that the comfortable Gospel of Christ may be truly preached, truly received, and truly followed, in all places, to the breaking down of the kingdom of Sin, Satan, and Death.' Convinced that, for the attainment of these blessed words, there must be some greater concert of action among Protestant Christians than any which yet exists, and believing that with you, Right Reverend Fathers, it rests to take the first measures tending thereto, your petitioners could not do less than humbly submit their Memorial to such consideration as in your wisdom you may see fit to give it. Praying that it may not be dismissed without reference to a commission, and assuring you, Right Reverend Fathers, of our dutiful veneration and esteem,

" We are, most respectfully,
" Your brethren and servants
" In the Gospel of Christ,
" W. A. MUHLENBERG,

C. F. Cruse, Philip Berry, Edwin Harwood, G. T. Bedell, Henry Gregory, Alex. H. Vinton, M. A. De Wolfe Howe, S. H. Turner, S. R. Johnson, C. W. Andrews, F. E. Lawrence," and others.[1]

The presentation of the subject as a memorial to the House of Bishops, rather than as a resolution in the lower house of the Convention, was an essential feature of the original design. Dr. Muhlenberg placed the highest estimate upon the episcopate, as a medium and an agency for catholic order. His own parish, the Holy Communion, was never represented in diocesan convention, for the reason that he did not approve of the constitution of those bodies; maintaining that a true council of the church should consist only of communicating members, and that, until such should be the case, all the conditions of Catholic fellowship were met, and all the ills of ecclesiastical politics avoided, by the union of each parish priest with his bishop. One chief

---

[1] It should be recorded in this connection that the Rev. Edwin Harwood, with Bishop Howe of Central Pennsylvania, and Bishop Bedell of Ohio, are the sole survivors of this once famous committee. To Dr. Harwood belongs the well-deserved honor of having edited with Dr. Muhlenberg *The Evangelical Catholic*, and of having been an efficient helper in establishing the system of the Episcopal Congress which has proved to be the first definite step towards realizing Muhlenberg's aspiration for the "unsectarizing of the church."

ground for his hope of a Catholic restoration lay in the possibility of inducing the bishops to inaugurate a movement looking toward their own emancipation from many of the customary restraints imposed upon their essential function by the unwritten law — or rather by the sectarian spirit — of the church. He urged the significance of the claim, that the church had both a catholic and a denominational character, and then proceeded to demonstrate, beyond all reasonable dispute, that the grand, catholic aspiration had been wholly lost in the mere sectarian business of developing, intensifying, exaggerating, and stereotyping her denominational peculiarities. Convincing proof of this was to be found in the admitted fact — in the case of some, the self-complacent boast — that she was the church of the rich, the respectable, the influential, and scarcely at all of the poor and the uncultured. This, he showed conclusively, was due to the settled system and policy of the church, which was utterly unadapted to the task that lay before her in this land, and which rigidly precluded such adaptation. She virtually claimed to be a church with a restricted mission, and was practically satisfied to remain such. And this was due to nothing inherent in her constitution, but to the unconscious growth of the sect spirit, which had fastened itself upon her. She had in her all the elements of catholicity, and it was to her proper development in this direction, as the norm of a catholic system, that he called the minds of her bishops in the bugle-blast of the Memorial. It proposed the initiation of measures looking toward a broader and more comprehensive field for the exercise of their great function; that, as the missionary agency of the church, to whom the great commission of the risen and ascended Lord comes with especial emphasis, they should mark out for their action as bishops, in admitting to the sacred ministry, a more catholic and comprehensive ground than that to which they were by custom then restricted. For a catholic church, including likewise denominational peculiarities, or distinctive practices in the minor details of worship and administration, to ordain men to the sacred ministry only on condition of their entire conformity to these lesser requirements, he held to be a contradiction in terms; and he demonstrated, with irresistible cogency and clearness of reasoning, the untenableness of all catholic pretensions in the face of such inconsistent practice. For himself, Dr. Muhlenberg had no quarrel with these peculiarities. He held to the necessity of the denomination in its individual organization, and to those who wished to give a pledge of conformity to its special requirements he would interpose no barrier. But to refuse ordination to the sacred ministry, or apostolic commission to preach the gospel and administer the sacraments orderly to those desiring it, who could not pledge conformity, he held to be not catholic, but sectarian. It savored not of that blessed liberty wherewith Christ hath made us free, but rather of that priestly tyranny which would lord it over God's heritage.

It was the hope, the possibility, and the practicability of a changed Episcopal attitude in this particular, that enabled him to see in the Episcopate a practicable basis of unity, or at least a medium and a bond of that catholic fellowship which must precede, and would surely prepare the way for, an organic unity that would be truly catholic. This is the high argument of his exposition of the Memorial, in support of the petition of the memorialists for the appointment of a permanent Episcopal commission on church unity. How skillfully he handled this line of reasoning the following extracts will barely indicate : —

" Any movement of this kind will be very apt to expose us to misunderstanding on the part of other denominations, perhaps to their ridicule. They will see in it only a vainglorious attempt of our bishops to magnify their office, if not an ambitious project to extend their fancied prerogative. We shall have the old stories over again of prelatical pride and tyranny. Very likely. The Memorial has been sneered at already in some quarters. Any action upon it may be sneered at much more. The thing will have to pass through a stage of misapprehension, probably misrepresentation and contempt. This will last for a while, and will proceed partly from those who really misconceive it, and partly from others who will not care to look at it aright. The religious journals, which live so much upon party and denominational prejudice, but which are far from representing the honest Christian sentiment of the communities to which they belong, will be busy, of course, in the line of their calling. All that is to be expected. In the mean while thoughtful men, sick at heart with the distractions and divisions among followers of the same Lord, will look at the matter dispassionately. They will perceive it is nothing sectarian, though emanating from what they call a sect. They will see that that sect stands on a vantage-ground peculiar to itself; they will see that it has something tangible and positive wherewith to proceed in measures for the peace of Christendom. They will reflect that it has adhered, with a tenacity beyond all other sects, to the ancient faith, in those ancient formulas which are the only basis that all can ever meet upon. These two things they will be constrained to admit : —

"1. In order to any effective union and intercommunion among the several Protestant bodies, each must have a ministry, the validity of which is acknowledged by all the others. 2. That none but a ministry episcopally ordained is thus acknowledged. This is a fact that cannot be denied, nor by any possibility can it be changed. Episcopal orders, and no others, admit everywhere to the pulpits of the Protestant faith. This is incontrovertible and immutable. Hence it will be seen that the Episcopal Church has an element of union at her disposal, and which she is now willing to diffuse on the most liberal terms. This is an idea not to be despised. Good and sensible men will think of it.

"They will come together to examine it, and to deliberate upon it. By degrees the first impressions on the minds of many will wear away.[1] Prejudice will yield to candor. Notions and feelings that were once believed to be sacred jealousy for the truth will reveal themselves as bigotry. Impartial judgment will begin to have place.[2] Let Episcopal orders be dispensed on the unsectarian conditions here contended for; let it be evident that the *first* concern of the bishop in giving them is for the propagation of the gospel, and his second for its propagation according to our forms; let the successors[3] of the apostles ordain men on the same terms as the apostles themselves ordained, and many will begin to reckon the value of Episcopal orders who now have never given a thought to the subject. Let them be fairly attain-

---

[1] These words read like a prophecy, uttered thirty years before their realization in the meetings of the Congress of Churches held at Hartford and Cleveland.

[2] *Evangelical Catholic Papers*, p. 150.

[3] "In order, if not in office." — (W. A. M.)

able, and they will be sought. The reasons for this opinion were expressed as follows some eighteen years ago : —

" 'The arguments for episcopacy would then be exhibited with more hopes of convincing its opponents, for then the question would be put upon its own merits. Now it is connected with various other matters, — the use of a certain liturgy, of peculiar rules and ceremonies, adherence to a particular ecclesiastical organization, etc. All these a man feels he must be ready for when he is convinced of episcopacy, if he is to turn his conviction to any practical account. Thus the cause has not the benefit of being tried alone. It is considered in connection with things that prejudice the judgment about it. But let it stand out disencumbered and on its own ground, let it be possible for a man to be an Episcopalian *quoad hoc,* and the controversy will not so often end, as it now does, with the confirmation of the parties in their respective opinions. Young men in the non-Episcopalian churches, preparing for the ministry, would examine the subject with more candor than can now be expected of them. Now they look upon Episcopal ordination as one of our peculiarities, — as part of what they call our sectarianism. Place it within reach on confessedly catholic terms, strip it of all unessential accessories, and they will look upon it with new eyes, — they will read the history of the early church over again, and review their own sectarian prejudices. Whatever might be their views of the necessity of Episcopal orders, they would be convinced of their high antiquity, and would desire them, if only from considerations of expediency, as the means of enlarging their field of labor.[1]

" ' Having received the ordination, they would reflect that they would be recognized as duly authorized ministers everywhere in the Protestant world. Missionaries, especially, would possess an immense advantage therein. In the many instances, it would open to them avenues of usefulness, from which without it they are excluded. Indeed, the advantages of Episcopal ordination are so obvious in many practical points of view, especially in regard to the missionary cause, that it cannot be doubted the more liberal and thoughtful men of other denominations would rise above party feeling, and recommend their young men to obtain it.' These sanguine hopes, entertained so long ago, still seem reasonable.[2]

. . . .

" The commission, until vested with powers not yet asked for it, would be no more than the authorized organ of communication with surrounding Christian

---

[1] " If it be said that Episcopal orders should not be given to men who have so low an estimate of their value, I would ask whether there be not those among ourselves who have no higher. How many thousand priests and deacons in the English Church have been ordained holding the extremest Low Church views! Besides, in the cases supposed, there would probably be an advance in the estimate of Episcopal ordination, as men generally value what they possess. At any rate, a belief in the apostolicity or antiquity of Episcopacy is not an article of the faith." — (W. A. M.)

[2] *Evangelical Catholic Papers*, pp. 126–128.

bodies or individuals sound in the faith. Such communication might issue in action, for which, however, the commission would require further instructions from the House of Bishops, or the whole Convention.

"Contemplating the result in the restoration of the evangelical commission to the Episcopate to be exercised in granting holy orders on evangelical terms, I argued for the commission, as the necessary *preparatory* measure, by showing how it should approve itself to both of the leading parties in the church, with the understanding that the commission would (until further orders) confine itself to *preliminary* or rather *tentative* action. I earnestly hope you will report in its favor. Discussing the proposition in conversation with many of our clergy and several of the bishops, I have found none to object to it, and most to give it their cordial assent. *Harm* it could do none. The *good* to which it might lead cannot be measured. At the least, it would be an *attempt*, an *essay* on the part of the only church which can make it with any prospect of success, to gather into one the sundered multitude of believers on the old ground of the one Lord, the one faith, the one baptism. Is not the ability of our church to put forth an effort to that end a talent, for the improvement of which she will be held responsible ? Shall she hide it in a napkin, — the napkin of her niceties and peculiarities?

"Our church (as is shown in a recent admirable charge by one of your brethren) has both a catholic and denominational character. Which shall we now

seek to develop ? This, in reference to *all* the wants
of the memorialists, is the question before you in
making up your report. If it be her denominational
character that she is most concerned for, your report
may be very brief. Dismiss the Memorial. Take
your stand on the prudential maxim, 'Let well alone.'
Our well-doing church will continue to do well in her
own sphere and peculiar mission; with her stern integrity, her conservative policy, her refined taste and
dignified bearing, she will always be most acceptable
in the upper walks of life, where, indeed, as well as
in the lower, there are souls to be gathered into the
kingdom; while, also, she will always have a goodly
number of retainers in her *beneficiaries* among the
poor. As she is, she can thus prosper; confessedly
the most respectable denomination in the land. But
if, without compromising any real advantages in that
character, she is mainly bent on developing the Catholic elements in her constitution, then give her ample
room for so glorious a mission. Bid her look over
this vast continent, filling with people of all nations,
and languages, and tongues, and see the folly of hoping to perpetuate among them an *Anglican* Communion that will ever be recognized as aught more than
an honorable sect; bid her give over the vain attempt
to cast all men's minds into one mould. Bid her
cherish among her own members mutual tolerance of
opinion in doctrine and taste in worship; remembering that uniform sameness in lesser matters may be
the ambition of a society, a party, a school, in the
church, but is far below any genuine aspirations of

the church herself. It is the genius of Catholicism which is now knocking at her doors. Let her refuse to open. Let her, if she will, make them faster still with new bolts and bars, and then take her rest, to dream a wilder dream than any of the Memorial, — of becoming the Catholic Church of the United States." [1]

By way of illustrating the actual attitude of the church on this question, in contrast with what he proposed, he supposes the following case of a non-conformist suing for orders at the hands of a bishop : —

" Let us say he is a good man. He believes himself moved by the Holy Ghost to give himself to furthering the salvation of his fellow - men. Besides the inward call, he wants the outward form of admission to the ministry, and respectfully craves it of the bishop. He has not thought of becoming just an Episcopal priest or deacon. He has had education enough to preach only to plain people. Besides, he wants sometimes to pray without a book. He thinks he has some gift in prayer (and I suppose there *is* such a thing). He is ready to give the bishop security for his adherence to the faith, the sacraments, and good order of the gospel, but he has not mastered every point of the Thirty-nine Articles, and fears he might be a little awkward in regulating himself by our rubrics and customs. He has been a Methodist man, and likes many of the Methodist ways better

[1] *Evangelical Catholic Papers*, pp. 323–325.

than ours. He believes much good is done in the class meetings, and would like to have them among the people wherever he was stationed. Still he has read enough to be satisfied that on the whole the safest and surest way of getting in the gospel ministry is to be put there by a bishop of the old line, and accordingly begs the favor of the nearest father in God in his neighborhood. But the father won't own him for a son unless he will give up all his 'Methodist notions,' betake himself to studying the Prayer Book, promise never to open his lips in public worship except in its identical words, and moreover will get a certificate of character from twelve Episcopalians, with whom the poor man would have to form an acquaintance for the first time ; the father in effect bids him to be gone to his meeting, and there get such ordination as he can : which is all very well, quite consistent, *provided* that the whole of the bishop's concern is to take care of the Protestant Episcopal Church ; that to look after her interests and seek her extension is the sum and substance of the Master's injunction, to which the bishop refers for his power." [1]

---

[1] *Evangelical Catholic Papers*, pp. 124, 125. High Churchmen would deny that they anathematize their orthodox nonepiscopal brethren, — that *would be* uncharitable. They only unchurch them. What *is* this unchurching? What does it amount to, as to the Christian estimate in which it obliges them to hold their unchurched brethren ? Very little. I have never yet known a churchman, however extreme in his views, much distressed at the death of pious Presbyterian relatives or friends, as doubting their salvation because they were not in

Further on, in continuing the subject entitled, " What the Memorialists Want," Dr. Muhlenberg writes as follows : —

"We do not look upon the orthodox Protestants around us as apostates from the faith. They accept the Apostles' and Nicene Creeds.[1] We have no Protestant Episcopal creed which we make, as Rome does hers, of equal authority with those ancient symbols, and which we call upon men to receive in order to admission to our pale. No ; it is for canons and rubrics, for rites and ceremonies, which the General Convention might sweep away to-morrow and our integrity as a church remain, that we are willing to

the church. Not so the sincere Romanist. One dear to him, dying out of the church, is an intense grief, and he gives all he can afford in masses for the restoration of the unfortunate soul. With us, all baptized, true Christian men are undoubtedly saved. If consistently with our dogma we cannot embrace them in the Catholic Church, we yet have a place for them in the communion of saints, so that practically the necessity of union with an Episcopal ministry, after all, we make of no great account. It does not affect salvation. Is it, then, only one of our tenets, or, in popular language, one of our "denominational peculiarities " ? and for no more than that do we ignore our brethren ? If we refuse the hand of fellowship to those whom, we have no doubt at all, we shall enjoy to meet hereafter at least, shall we not consent to a consideration of the practicability of recognizing that brotherhood on earth which we shrink from saying will not exist in heaven ?

[1] But *how* do they accept them ? you say. Quite as freely and heartily as many among ourselves whom you do not repudiate as heretics, — with whom you are in constant communion. — (W. A. M.)

leave Christian neighbors and kinsmen to the 'uncovenanted mercies of God,' the same that we award to the virtuous heathen.

"The sum of the whole is this — the Episcopate is either a catholic or a peculiar institution. It is essential, or it is not, to the being of the church. If it be the latter, while we adhere to it for all the good we derive from it ourselves, let us not, as we would keep the unity of spirit and bond of peace, make it a cause of division in the household of faith. Away with every law or rule that magnifies its importance at so fearful a rate! If it be the former, an essential of the Catholic Church, then, in the name of Him who ordained it as such, and who prayed that his followers might be one, let us be sure that we dispense its blessings far and wide on the most liberal terms. Freely as we have received, freely let us give, else the sin will lie at our doors of breaking the unity of the Body of Christ.

"Either party on the question of episcopacy among us is inconsistent in maintaining the present state of things, — one in recognizing brethren in their neighbor Christians, yet shunning contact with them, on no ground of principle, for expediency's sake, or, perchance, lest the respectability of the church should suffer; the other, in its zeal for every iota of our Church's prescriptions, narrowing her down to the dimensions of a sect. Both have the leaven, in different forms, of the old Judaistic spirit which troubled the church at first. It has appeared in every age, at once the life and the poison of sect. Alas that it should be rife among ourselves!

" The foregoing, I shall be told, seems to proceed on the assumption that there are ministers in the orthodox denominations who are desirous of obtaining Episcopal orders ; that they are suing at our doors for the boon which, in order to its being thankfully accepted, we have only to grant. By no means. The reverse may be the fact ; nay, the idea of their lacking anything in their ministry which we could supply may only be treated with contempt by most of our nonepiscopal brethren. Be it so ; it does not touch the point. The question is, what should be our attitude towards them, not theirs to us. At present it is one of repulsion on both sides. We prohibit intercourse, and they consequently eschew it. But let us change our attitude, so far at least as to show a readiness to ascertain whether a better understanding is not possible. That, if it does not alter our relations, will not fail to improve the temper of them. But whether it does or not, we shall have acquitted ourselves, we shall have done our duty. Results do not determine duties. Though it could be foreseen that the advance on our part would be met by none on the part of others, — nay, that it would be scorned, — it would still be ours to make the advance. Let the commission be appointed, — let it be actuated by the spirit of gospel peace, — and then, whatever comes of it, though it seem but idle and abortive for the while, the church will have nothing to regret. It will be hers to say, *Liberavi animam meam.*"

This crucial question of ordination was the

supreme difficulty requiring the most careful adjustment in any proposed scheme of Christian union, which his intuitive mind had seized upon as early as the year 1835, eighteen years before the Memorial Movement was inaugurated, when he published a little volume entitled "Hints on Catholic Union," and to which the slow-plodding masses of Christendom turned indifferent ears. Another point in this book which displayed that wonderful insight, amounting at times to accurate prevision, which characterized his mind, was the expediency of an "inter-ecclesiastical congress" as a means of arriving at a due understanding of differences and practical adjustment of difficulties. Concerning this matter of ordination, in this little volume he speaks as follows : —

"The only possible way of removing the obstacle appears to be this : In a council of representatives from the various churches, assembled to debate the matter, let it be agreed to adopt that form of ordination, or conveyance of the external commission to the ministry, *which all believe to be sufficient, and not repugnant to the word of God*. In order to accomplish this, the sufficiency and non-contrariety to the word of God, of the proposed ordination, must be the only question considered. There must be no inquiry which ordination is the most apostolical, or which the most like that of the primitive church, which the most excellent ; for on these questions every one would have his own views, and of course would contend for them, and thus there would be a repetition of the old and endless controversies with which the church has long enough been perplexed. The single point to be determined should be, what form of ordination is acknowledged to be valid by all, and may be received by all without any sacrifice of conscience. If no such ordination can be found, union is impossible. If there cannot be a cordial admission of the due authority of one another's ministry by the several churches, it is evident they must remain asunder. But the requisite ordination, it is believed, may be found. Let Episcopalians, Presbyterians, and Congregationalists meet harmoniously and compare their views. Let them canvass the question in the spirit of brotherly love, and honestly endeavor to discover some ground of peace and union. Let them consent to substitute, in place of what they now prefer, any form of ordination in which all could conscientiously unite, and they would not be long in coming to a decision."

In a note to this passage he further adds : [1] —

" The question of the sufficiency of ordination could not be determined by the plurality of voices in the

---

[1] " A suggestion in passing, upon this vexing question, is here made, — namely, whether the power and value of a genuine ordination for a reconstructed ministry may not, after all, be found to inhere in a syndicate, or ecclesiastical commission, in which a clerical member of each religious body shall contribute his special form of ordination by the laying-on of hands." — *The Vine Out of Egypt*, p. 115.

council, for the conscience of no *one* must be violated. The majority could not change the minority's views of truth. The problem to be solved is, what is expedient in the exigency, and lawful in the eyes of all? Any arguments of divine origin or superior antiquity would only throw the council into interminable discussion." [1]

Thus far concerning the emancipation of the Episcopate. All this, let us observe, was regarded by Dr. Muhlenberg as involved in the church's simple fulfillment of her Lord's great commission to "preach the gospel to every creature." All this he held to be inseparably implicated in her plain duty to declare the manifold wisdom of God to all sorts and conditions of men, — or, in modern phrase, "to reach the masses." So clearly do the simplest duty and the nearest practical results involve the highest aim in order to their fulfillment and realization!

As to the grand result, toward which the Memorial Movement was designed to contribute, Dr. Muhlenberg's faith never faltered; his zeal and effort never flagged; he believed in the Catholic reunion of dismembered Christendom. He had no patience with the complacent cant which apologizes for the sins of division and strife, on the plea that each denomination is a division of the Lord's army, called to do a special

[1] *Evangelical Catholic Papers*, pp. 21, 22.

kind of work, each excelling in its own line of effort, and best achieving the proper result in its own way. He believed the Saviour's promise to his disciples, " Lo, I am with you alway, even to the end of the world." He believed that He who gave this promise is not the author of confusion, but of peace ; and that where envy and strife is, there is nought but confusion and every evil work ; and believing also that judgment should begin at the house of God, he strove first of all to convince his own communion of her share of blame in this matter, and to purge her from the demon of sect, as a first step toward the far-off consummation. In the following passage Dr. Muhlenberg has clearly and powerfully sketched the evils incident upon the present divisions of Christians : —

" Among the various sources of hope for greater agreement ere long among Protestant Christians, there is one arising from the fact of their common zeal for the extension of the gospel among the heathen. This zeal is very strongly characteristic of the leading evangelical denominations, and has been, with increasing energy, for the last fifty years. It is decided and persevering, and never has been more so than at the present. Never did men give more freely of their money to missions ; never were there larger numbers of evangelists in the foreign field. What has been the result ? Success enough to encourage the continuance of effort, but by no means adequate to expectation. On the contrary there has been disappointment. The results bear no satisfactory proportion to the means and agencies employed. This would appear on a reference to the principal missionary societies both here and in England, but that is unnecessary. The failure is acknowledged, — failure compared with what was looked for. We have only to recollect the confident anticipations, from time to time, of the conversion of regions all ready for the gospel, if only the means were forthcoming, if only Christians would pray as they ought. The means were not stintedly given ; the "monthly concert of prayer" did not cease ; but the hoped-for regions are in the realms of darkness still. While, again, there are bright pages in the history of missions, cheering tokens that the good Lord does not disown the labors of his servants, yet on the whole there has been in a human point of view so much of discouragement that still to persevere in the work, still to prosecute it with vigor, is felt to be a trial of their faith, a test of their obedience. As good Christians they are willing to go on in faith, they are content simply to obey. At the same time they cannot help inquiring why it is so. Wherefore is so much of their toil apparently in vain ? Why are their hopes so long postponed ? With all their zeal, their efforts, their prayers, may there not be still some fault of their own which explains the disappointment, and they are beginning to suspect what it is ? Here and there, they are beginning to see it. It is becoming plain to their eyes. *They are not at peace among themselves.* This is their fault, their grievous fault.

They are not at peace among themselves. While they would proclaim the gospel of peace abroad, they are disputing in fierce contentions with one another what that gospel is. They substitute their systems for the gospel, and spend their strength in propagating their systems. Zealous only for the divine glory, as they have fondly believed, they see they have been more anxious to plant the flag of their divisions on the pagan soil than the banner of the Lord of Hosts. The spirit of sect, — this is 'the accursed thing' for which discomfiture has awaited the armies of the Lord. 'This is the cause why the inhabitants of the earth have not fallen before the Cross. The sin is ours. God hath called us to be workers together with Him, to make known to man the privileges and the glory of belonging to his family. He gave us his gospel that we might live as a united family, serving Him and one another, and, being such a family, He bade us go forth and preach the gospel to every creature, saying He would be with us to the end of the world. We have not chosen to be such a family; we have not chosen to live as those who are united in a crucified Saviour; we have mocked our own words when we would call upon men to become members with us of the one household of faith; the words of life and power from our lips have been like the utterances of men in their dreams; there has been a spot in our feasts of charity.' [1]

" Nay, we *have* no feasts of charity. That highest feast of charity, the Holy Supper, is no longer a feast

[1] F. D. Maurice.

at which Christians meet simply as Christians, and as fellow-disciples of a common Lord. There is not one table, but one hundred tables, table against table ; the partakers of each practically saying theirs alone is the table of the Lord. We are thus separated from one another in this supreme and distinctive act of our religion, the very sign and means of our communion in Christ. We partake apart, as locally we must, but it is more than difference of place that hinders a realization of the unity which it is the very design of this ordinance of love to set forth and confirm. We will not, we cannot, go to one another's communions ; we refrain on principle ; we are kept back by our respective systems of doctrine or practice, which we thus virtually exalt to a higher value than the common faith. Here is a fact sufficient in itself to demonstrate the hatefulness of the sect spirit. We eschew one another's company at the table of Jesus Christ, and that, alas ! for conscience' sake ! As long as this lasts, in vain shall we hope to convert the unbelieving world. What ! try to persuade men to come and be children with us of the Almighty Parent, while we are not in amity enough ourselves to meet at the board of his dear and only Son ! Teach them to say, 'Our Father, who art in heaven,' while we will not come together as brethren in his house to unite in the prayer ! No wonder we fail ! No surprise do the angels feel that they have so little cause for rejoicing at the conversion of the heathen sinners, while they see so much of Christians at variance. In his mercy the Lord blesses the ministrations of his word and

ordinances among us, but as to our efforts to publish
his name abroad, which should be sounded forth with
the full harmony of concordant voices, He leaves us to
the consequences and punishment of our divisions.
He is not with us. He does not make bare his arm,
as for his people of old. Graciously He deigns to
continue to us his presence, but with no manifesta-
tions of its ancient glory and power. For the love He
beareth us, with all our undeservings, He gives us
pastors and teachers; He suffers not a famine of the
Word; but He raises up no prophets, 'mighty in word
and deed before the people.' Trumpets in his name
have been blown long and loud; priests have made
their processions seven times, and seven times again:
but the walls of Jericho have not fallen down. So it
will continue, to our confusion, more or less, until the
hosts of the Lord, merging their feuds in the one
grand strife for the honor of his name, shall go forth
as one man ' to the help of the Lord, to the help of
the Lord against the mighty.' Peace there must be
in the Lord's house, ere it be 'established on the top
of the mountains and the nations flow unto it.' The
dews of divine charity must descend for the refreshing
and renewing of Zion, drawn down by the 'one heart
and the one mind' of those who long for her prosper-
ity, ere the 'wilderness and the solitary places' beyond her 'will be made glad, or the deserts rejoice
and blossom as the rose.' It was when men said of
Christians, 'Behold how they love one another,' that
the church was mighty to the pulling down of the
strongholds of Satan; and again must Christians be

bound together in active fellowship, ere they avail, with aught of pristine strength, against his dominions in heathendom now.

" And if Protestant Christianity, from the want of combined forces, thus fails of conquest abroad, how largely also from the same cause does it fall short of its true power in its mission of beneficence at home, and in grappling with its foes of infidelity, superstition, and worldliness all about it, and on the ground which it claims as its own ! See the great and good works which it has to leave undone ; see the glorious enterprises of charity and benevolence which, from want of unanimity among its disciples, it has not the strength to undertake ; see the universities, the colleges, the hospitals, the manifold institutions of mercy for every form of human want and woe, which, if it could act with a common will, it would rear to the glory of its Lord, but which are now reared only on condition that they shall recognize no form of religion, which is tantamount to their recognizing no religion at all ! See how it has to abandon the rising generation of the masses, handing over their education to the state, that knows not Christ ; see how impotent it is in controlling public opinion ; how it fails to infuse a Christian spirit into literature and art ; see what an unequal match it is, with its militia regiments, against the disciplined hosts of a pseudo-Christianity ; see the advantage it yields the infidel to make capital out of its jealousies, contentions, and mutual recriminations, and tauntingly to ask, if he were minded to be a Christian, which of its hundred conflicting forms should he accept; and all because the arch-enemy has been allowed to act on the successful stratagem, in every kind of warfare, *divide and conquer!* Things will prove no better; Protestant Christianity will become no more effective in its foreign or domestic operations until its various bodies, in their sound elements, combine in tangible and practical union, not in identity of form or of discipline, or modes of worship or sentiment, in which Christians will differ as long as all minds are not cast in one mould and not exposed to the same influence and circumstances, but in an embodiment of those great evangelic and catholic principles of which it is the characteristic that they constitute unity in the midst of variety. The church, the congregation of baptized believers, to be found among all communions that hold fellowship in the Divine Head, must be manifested as such. It must be seen in its normal state, as the Brotherhood in Christ, — the one Divine Fraternity on earth, — the society of all who are sealed with the sacrament of adoption, and who own themselves, as thereby declared, brethren, because God is their Father, through the eternal Son, made their brother in the flesh, and ever dwelling in their midst by the power of the Holy Ghost. This is the Catholic Church. Let this Catholicity be owned and have sway; let there be Catholic hearts, and souls, and minds, to give life and energy to the profession of the Catholic Creed; let theological dogmata, schools, and platforms be put back to their legitimate place, to make room for a restoration of the ' Catholic Consent,' in the substance

of the faith; let all but confess to that; let all but
agree in the person and offices of our Blessed Lord,
as the God-man, the Prophet, Priest, and King, the
one Meditator between God and man, the final Judge
of the quick and dead, who will render to every man
according to his works; let the right hand of fellowship be withheld from none to whom He is thus 'All
and in All;' and (returning to our subject), let those
who, in virtue of their ancient office, may be foremost
in promoting so blessed a consummation, seriously lay
it to heart, and inquire what action may be taken
thereto; let all others view the effort Christianly,
judge it impartially, construe it charitably, and a
work will have been begun deserving the benediction
of all good men, and, with their benediction, will not
end until the church, spoiled by the demon of sect no
more, shall be hailed as the city of God, the joy of
the whole earth. Amen."

The memorialists also craved some modifica-
tions in the method of worship prescribed by the
church, in order to its better adaptation to the
character of the people and the wants of the
time. They held that changes in this direction
were imperative, — if the church was to gain
any permanent and general hold on the masses
of the people. Their complaint was, not that
the liturgy was made three hundred years ago
for the English people, among whom the intelligence of the masses, their wants and social con-

dition, were vastly different from those encoun-
tered in this new America, but that its offices
had been cramped and crystallized into an unmeaning routine; and that it was no longer recognized as a living system capable of growth
and adaptation to the people.   In the words of
one of these writers: —

"We were the colonial daughter of England when as
yet no American nation was born, and that original
type has never changed; but while Presbyterian and
Puritan have adapted themselves to the nation, we
have been and are a stereotype copy of England still.
The changes of the church should be like those of
nature, which does not lop off a branch, but puts forth
an inward power replacing the withered with the
new; and the same oneness will no more produce the
same worship for every land and age than the same
tree will have entire uniformity in every climate and
soil.[1]

"The difficulty lies not so much in the liturgy itself
as in our too rigid use of it; it is absolutely imperative in every detail amidst all the changing circumstances of ministerial work.   We are so far from
conservative in this that we have lost its original
method; we have not at all the varied hours and
varied offices of those who framed the liturgy.   It
was never meant to be the same routine for all occasions; we have made it such, and deadened it by
our own stiffness.   Devotion wearies with the repe-

---

[1] Quoted in *Evangelical Catholic Papers*, pp. 277, 278.

tition morning and evening, not only the Lord's day
but on every day, of the same form of ' linked sweetness long drawn out.'   But the defect is felt far more
with the missionary, among those who have not the
trained habit of worship.   Imagine St. Paul harangu-
ing the crowd of Athens or Lystra, in every discourse
at every fresh station beginning with his ' Dearly beloved brethren ' ; reading Venite and Te Deum when
he found no music ; making his own responses ; and so
through Litany and Ante-Communion, service on service, Ossa on Pelion, before he could speak one hearty
word of the kingdom of God !   It is no caricature.
Not a missionary meeting in Western wilds, not a
handful of countrymen untrained in liturgies, but
hungering after truth, can listen without these pre-
liminaries." [1]

On this head Dr. Muhlenberg himself has the
following pregnant paragraph : —

" The object of this section is simply to impose the
liturgy only where it can be employed as a real service, which can be nowhere but in assemblies of people professedly Christian, and who know how to use
it.   I need not say that it is designed for no others.
A prayer-book is made for people who pray ; ours is
made for those who are prepared to pray according
to its goodly order.   But how often, in a country like
this, must the preacher present himself before those
who are unprepared to pray after any fashion, and
who need to be taught the first principles of prayer !

[1] *Evangelical Catholic Papers*, p. 279.

And yet, whatever be the character of the hearers, he must begin with the book, and proceed as it directs, for the canon makes no exception in his favor, — 'Every minister,' etc.[1] Of course common sense intervenes. He does the best under the circumstances. He remembers that necessity has no law, and yet he feels that he is under law. He has a sense of obligation to canonical and rubrical requirements. He has promised obedience to them; hence he feels it his duty at once to introduce the prayer-book, and use it as far as he possibly can. He instructs the people in its order of worship. To this he gives himself as a necessary and preliminary work. Thus it happens that our missionaries (I speak of those in our own country) so seldom appear simply as evangelists. They may feel that they are such, and sincerely desire to be recognized in that character; but they are not thus recognized. From the mode of action to which they are constrained by what is expected of them, and by what they consider obedience to the church, the people look upon them not so much as preachers of Christ's Gospel as ministers of a particular denomination sent out to make converts to

---

[1] " To be consistent, Episcopalians ought, of all Christians, to have the most faith in sudden conversions. Let the gathering at which one of our clergy officiates be what it may, of the ignorant and unbaptized, of infidels or scoffers, he must needs fancy that all at once they have become the dearly beloved in Christ, penitent believers, ready to fall on their knees in confession, to receive absolution, and lift up their hearts and voices in the adoration of saints! Is such an *opus operatum* the doctrine of any school among us ? " — (W. A. M.)

it. Their object, whatever it really is, appears to be
to Episcopalianize rather than evangelize their hearers. How can it be otherwise? For what is the
frequent course of the missionary, accustomed all his
previous life to the order of the church, and with the
vows of his ordination fresh upon him to obey the
statute for that order? He goes to a neighborhood
to which he is attracted by hearing of Episcopalians
there. He hunts them up. He appoints a service,
inviting the inhabitants of the place generally to
attend. Perchance he has come across some staunch
old churchman who boasts that, in all his exile from
Zion, he has never once seen the inside of a 'meeting-
house,' and who is now only too glad to act the clerk.
With a respondent on hand, what hinders their having
the whole service? And so they have it; the good
folk who have come to hear 'a preaching' staring at
the two performers ever and anon going through a
dialogue. Now, without inquiring how much of the
'beauty of holiness' they are likely to discern in such
an exhibition, I would ask whether any distinct idea
is likely to be conveyed to them of the missionary as
the herald of salvation? Do they not shrewdly guess
among themselves that he has come to try and make
'Episcopals' of them?[1] God speed every effort to

[1] "The above is no fancy sketch. When a lay reader, in my
youth, I have acted in such a performance. One of our clergy,
who spent a part of his life, and nearly the whole of his fortune, in planting the church in the West, has told me how the
missionary bishop and he would go to places and advertise
public worship in a court-house or school-room, where the
bishop and he would conduct the service according to canon

extend our apostolic church, with her comely order, with her ritual rich in evangelic truth, her inheritance from the saints of better days! God rear everywhere her altars, centres of her saving light, throughout the land! God prosper her, lengthening her cords, and strengthening her stakes, the best hope of the world! But has she no confidence in herself? No confidence in herself as a church of Christ? With all her professions has she still misgivings whether she be a church of Christ, doubting his care of her, unless, by her looking well to all and the least of her works and defenses, she first takes care of herself? Is she afraid to go alone in the power of God? Dare she never elevate the cross save amid the walls and battlements of her own erection? Must she always seem to make things divine and human in her constitution, things great and small, of equal moment? Must she be strenuous for the mint, anise, and cumin the moment she opens her mouth on the weightier matters of law? Granting all that is said of her glorious adornments, daughter of Israel is she, and must she believe that the King can have no pleasure in her beauty unless arrayed in her full dress, — 'in her

and rubric, with not a voice in the congregation but their own; while, perhaps, in the same places, the Roman bishop would come along, call the people together, begin at once with a familiar address, and end with a short prayer. Which left the most favorable impression on the people's minds? Which pursued the better policy for his own church? The Jesuit, knowing *ars est celare artem*, or our honest bishop and chaplain putting on an appearance of sectarianism which they did not feel?" — *Evangelical Catholic Papers.*

clothing (so be it) of wrought gold'? Such has been too much her mistaken policy. The constraints of the canon, as it stands, are part of the policy. We ask that they be put out of the way. We ask that her evangelists may be suffered to be evangelists in the simple work of their office. We ask that ministers of the Protestant Episcopal Church, when going forth as missionaries, may go forth as ministers of the Catholic Church, — as preachers of the Lord Jesus Christ. Let it be seen — let it be patent to all men — that they are the heralds of the gospel to sinners, whose acceptance of it is the one burden of their souls, the one prayer and desire of their hearts. Let not that be obscured by their having to put forward any other interest which they may thus seem to have equally at heart. In all their ways and modes of operations let that which really is be also seen to be their high aim. Let them go forth in the living power of the truth, assured that the love of the truth, wherever it is received, will accept of all things needful for its conservation, its appliance, and extension.[1]

"That will be to begin at the beginning. We must first give glory to God ere He will glorify us, even in the building of his Church. We must glorify

---

[1] "The present method of procedure, by which the Episcopalianism of our missionaries is put foremost and made so prominent, excites opposition, which of course adds to their obstructions. Often controversial tracts are distributed, which only serve to inform those otherwise ignorant, how much can be said against the church." — (W. A. M.)

his Son Jesus. We must set Him forth in the simple grandeur and all-sufficiency of his offices, ere we can hope He will own our work, or bless it as done in his name. It is upon this, first and foremost, our hearts, our minds, and souls must be intent, losing sight for the while of other things, though we believe them subservient to this. Let these latter come in due time, in their proper order, and He whom we glorify will make room for them so as we have first acquitted ourselves to Him. We may preach the church full zealously, work for it, and think we have established it, and still have to look in vain for the shekinah on the altar."

These animated expressions of personal conviction were conveyed to the public in a succession of powerful pamphlets, which attracted wide attention and elicited vehement discussion. The first was entitled an " Exposition of the Memorial," and was distinguished for clearness of language, vigorous argument, and copious illustration. For greater definiteness of statement, and the clearing away of misapprehensions and misconstructions, this was followed by two others, under the respective titles of " What the Memorialists Want," and " What the Memorialists do not Want." These all appear in Dr. Muhlenberg's collected works, under the title of " Evangelical Catholic Papers."

How great the need was, in the Protestant

Episcopal Church of that day, of such an awakening as that of the Memorial Movement, may
be judged by the following extract from a final
communication of Dr. Muhlenberg on the Memorial : —

FURTHER COMMUNICATION ON THE MEMORIAL.

*To the Rt. Rev. Bishop Otey, Chairman of the
Commission of Bishops.*

"RIGHT REVEREND AND DEAR SIR, — Allow me
to say a few words in regard to my recent letter which
I ventured publicly to address to yourself. Great
has been my surprise at the comments which it has
called forth in various and opposite quarters. I
fondly hoped that the dread which was expressed of
mischief to the church, lurking in the vague terms
of the Memorial, would be quite allayed when distinct statements were put forth of 'What the Memorialists Want,' — so reasonable and moderate did I
deem them, and such I am persuaded they would
be *generally* deemed were they calmly and candidly
considered. Instead of that, or of any temperate
discussion of the several points at issue, there has
been a rejection of the whole, and in language so
denunciatory that I can account for it only by sup-
posing that its authors, having made up their minds
beforehand, did not care to construe fairly, much less
charitably, what they felt bound to condemn. Such
is not the way to treat views and sentiments bearing
on the interests of the church, entertained by her

acknowledged well-wishers, and honestly exhibited for her good. To brand them as 'mischievous,' 'revolutionary,' 'heretical,' etc., is scarcely enough. Something like proof should be attempted."

More might be quoted from this second communication of Dr. Muhlenberg's, were it necessary, but the above is sufficient to show the inflamed and acrimonious spirit in which the Memorial was received by those to whom it was with so much loyal confidence addressed. If the immediate results of the Movement were somewhat disappointing to Dr. Muhlenberg, yet, in the light of subsequent history, he builded even better than he knew. But the immediate fruits of the venture were more than could have been reasonably hoped for, in the existing state of feeling and thought in the church: the whole body was aroused to a wholesome review of the stereotyped formalism and inflexible conservatism into which, from long isolation, it had fallen. It was led to see that apostolic claims alone were futile in the absence of the catholic spirit and missionary fervor, with suitable flexibility and adaptiveness of method. Dr. Muhlenberg was the unquestioned reviver of the genuine catholic temper in the American Church; and whatever advances we have seen in the direction of catholic freedom, tolerance, and charity, in the last fifty years, have been due to

him more than to any other person or influence.
There were also more tangible results at the
time. In the General Convention of 1856, the
bishops passed their famous declaration to the
effect that the order of Morning Prayer, the
Litany, and the Communion Service, being three
separate offices, may, as in former times, be used
separately. The declaration proceeded to give
authority to the bishops to prepare services
suitable for congregations not acquainted with
nor accustomed to the use of the Book of Common Prayer, and a commission on church unity
was appointed "as an organ of communication
or conference with such Christian bodies or
individuals as may desire it." This commission
accomplished nothing worthy of mention, and
was soon discharged.

It is strange to realize that this commission
could find nothing practical to do upon such a
subject. But we must remember that Dr. Muhlenberg was fully thirty years before his time,
and, being so, he sowed the potent seed which is
yielding its rich fruitage to-day. "Every man
in his own order." All the liturgical freedom
asked for in the Memorial is now virtually
gained; and what advances of Christian sentiment are being made toward organic catholic
unity we know. But all are not aware how far
and how directly this very progress is due to

Dr. Muhlenberg and the Memorial Movement. Yet the whole chain of historic sequences is traceable directly to his influence. Let the following serve as an illustration.

The Congress of Churches, and the subsequent declaration of the House of Bishops at Chicago in 1886, are matters of present-day history, and constitute the only tangible and historic achievements in the direction of church unity, since the Memorial Movement, registering a very decided advance in Christian sentiment upon the subject.[1] Such a declaration as that of the bishops, in 1886, would have abundantly satisfied Dr. Muhlenberg, and embodies substantially all that he contended for in the Memorial, yet it was impossible of attainment in his day. Like Abraham of old, he longed to see such a day of the Lord, and with true prophetic vision he saw it and was glad. How the realization of that far-off dream was brought about as a result of his own labors, the following, from the opening address by the Rev. Joseph Anderson, D. D., in the American Congress of Churches at Hartford, 1885, will show : —

"In the course of his reading, an Episcopal rector came in contact with the project of Dr.

[1] Much has been written upon the subject of unity, but these two facts are the only historic events which record definite action upon this subject.

Muhlenberg [to establish a council or congress of churches, with a view to healing the divisions of Christendom], to which reference has been made; and the question arose in his mind, ' Is it not possible that the grand dream of this man may yet be realized?' Without long delay, he gave this thought to the world through the press. He published an article in the 'Christian Union' on measures for the promotion of unity, in which he said, ' Let steps be taken toward an inter-ecclesiastical congress on the same plan as the English or American Congress of the Episcopal Church. Let it be held in the spring of the year, and let it take the place of the May anniversaries, which were once a power, but are now only a memory. Let representatives, lay and clerical, come to a central meeting place, not to vote, nor to preach, nor to exercise ecclesiastical function, but to tell of what they have, and what they lack.'

" But the Christian ministers of that neighborhood were already an inter-ecclesiastical congress on a small scale. They were noted in all the region for their hearty coöperation in every good work. These men were easily brought together, and this project was laid before them. This was on the 10th of November, 1883, the four hundredth anniversary of the birth of Luther. The result of this interview was a circular, brief and unpretentious, entitled ' A Call for an Inter-Ecclesiastical Church Congress.' It spoke of the possibility of organizing a movement which should be, to the different religious bodies of Protestant Christendom, very much what the Episcopal Church Congress had been to the Episcopal Church in uniting the different schools of thought contained in it. ' All attempts in the past,' it said, ' such as that represented by the Evangelical Alliance, have failed, because they have endeavored to ignore differences instead of affirming positive convictions.' It was something very different that was now proposed, and it seemed good to these brethren to take this initiatory step in the matter of ' sounding the churches.'

" This circular, which had seven names appended to it, representing the four Protestant denominations of the place, was sent forth into all parts of the land, and called out a prompt and warm response. The heartiest approval of the project came from the Episcopal Church; but all the churches were heard from, and everybody seemed to feel that the time had come for this new step forward in the religious life of America. On New Year's Day, 1884, these ministers came together again to read the replies they had received, which numbered nearly two hundred. They were from eminent divines,

college presidents, and laymen prominent in
Christian work. And, while difficulties were
not overlooked by these thinkers, they all expressed their interest in the project, and most
of them bade it Godspeed.

"In view of this cordial response, measures
were taken for a conference of persons specially
interested in the movement. The conference
was held on the 18th of June, 1884. The attendance was not large, but it was fairly representative. After a full discussion of the whole
subject, it was unanimously decided that it was
expedient to carry forward the proposed movement in the direction indicated by the circulars
which had been published. It was agreed that
the new organization should be named 'The
American Congress of Churches,' and the purpose of the movement was formulated in the
words which have now become so familiar to us,
'to promote Christian union, and to advance
the kingdom of God, by a free discussion of
the great religious, moral, and social questions of
the time.' To the question, how the Congress
should be governed, a wise and simple answer
was returned. It was voted that the general
management of the organization should be intrusted to a committee or 'council,' numbering
twenty-five persons, in which both clergymen
and laymen should be represented; and it was

agreed that the signers of the circular, in response to which the conference had come together, should have a place in the council. Two other gentlemen who were present were added to the list, and this committee of eight was instructed to proceed to the appointment of the additional members, with the understanding that, as soon as fifteen members were secured, the council should be convened for the consideration of the work committed to it.

" The first meeting of the council was held in New Haven, on the 20th of November, last year. A permanent organization was then effected, and an executive committee of seven was appointed, to which was intrusted the task of preparing for the first meeting of the congress, and of deciding when and where it should be held, and what topics should be discussed. The work done since then has been done by this executive committee, and for the most part by the chairman and the secretary.

" If time permitted, an account might properly be given of an auxiliary movement which has been going on in the West, in the city of St. Louis, in which two members of the executive committee have taken some part. But we can only refer in the briefest way to the vote in approval of the American Congress of Churches passed at a meeting of the St. Louis ministers,

— more than thirty being present, — and to the invitation extended by them to the congress to hold its second meeting in that city.

"It is a fact in which we may well find satisfaction — a fact without parallel hitherto — that our congress had the offer of a second place of meeting, before the first meeting had assembled."[1]

Thus has this far-off dream of Dr. Muhlenberg become a living fact, so strangely does history verify the wisdom of God's prophets in all ages. And in this way it has come to pass that, an entire generation after the heroic labors of Dr. Muhlenberg, the potent seeds of his example which inspired it sprang up in the minds and hearts of younger men, and brought forth the only historic movement in the direction of his aims that has arisen since his venture for emancipating the Episcopate, and the unsectarizing of the Church.

But whether the " United Churches of the United States " is to be only a paper plan or a definite fact the future alone will reveal.

" All we have willed, or hoped, or dreamed of good shall exist,
Not its semblance, but itself: no beauty, nor good, nor power,

[1] *American Congress of Churches*, Hartford meeting, 1885, pp. 23, 24, 25.

Whose voice has gone forth, but each survives for the mel-
odist
When eternity confirms the conception of an hour.

"The high that proved too high, the heroic for earth too
hard,
The passion that left the ground to lose itself in the sky,
Are music sent up to God by the lover and the bard :
Enough that He heard it once, — we shall hear it by and
by."

ROBERT BROWNING, *Abt Vogler.*

THE GROWTH OF INSTITUTIONAL-
ISM THROUGH THE GENIUS
OF HIS PERSONALITY.

"The holy Catholic Church is the communion of saints. The life of the Spirit is the life of communion with God. It is not a communion which is measured by finite limitations, and it is not distant in place, nor remote in time. But the world is slow to receive this, and is concerned with its own nothingness and emptiness. This communion is transposed, or is held as the association of an adjourned company. It is foisted into the future, in that conception in which the things not seen are still apprehended as some future temporality, and the present is occupied only with some indefinite notions among its pure negations.

"This communion, by a sheer lift, is carried into another world, which is then only another world in the succession to this world. The vague aspiration which wearies of its own vacancy, and the imagination which lingers among the things that are seen, the things of earth and time, brings to this its own detachments.

"The writer of the Epistle to the Hebrews says, '*Ye are come unto this communion;*' it is not '*Ye shall* come to this communion.*'

"That is the revision of the skepticism of the world. The argument of the writer of the epistle is to show that the Christ has rent asunder the veil which separates the earth from the heavens, and those who are in the world from those who have left it. It is not a communion to which men are told that they shall come, nor can the imagination pass beyond these words: '*Ye are come unto the city of the living God, and to an innumerable company of angels, to the general assembly and church of the first-born, which are written in heaven, and to God, the Judge of all, and to the spirits of just men made perfect.*' These words embrace the whole realization of that historical life: '*Ye are come unto Mount Zion, and unto the heavenly Jerusalem, and unto Jesus, the Mediator of the new covenant.*'" — MULFORD, *The Republic of God.*

CHAPTER V.

THE GROWTH OF INSTITUTIONALISM THROUGH THE GENIUS OF HIS PERSONALITY.

IN his essay upon " The Church as a Teacher of Morality," the author of " Ecce Homo," Professor Seeley, of Cambridge, England, uses these words : —

" Upon the question whether the Christian community is regarded by its teachers as one and homogeneous, or as divided between a small number of believers, the children of light, and a large number of merely nominal believers, — the disguised children of darkness, — depends, more than is commonly perceived, the whole character of Christian teaching. Those teachers who take the latter view will practically abandon all moral questions ; those who take the former will occupy themselves as much with morality as with religion.

" That the High Church party, who have generally shrunk much more than the Evangelicals from drawing the perilous line of demarcation, have, nevertheless, not occupied themselves much more with moral questions, is due to such a counteracting influence. They have been, for the most part, conservatives, attached by temper and tradition to the existing order of things, both political and social. They have been disposed to regard all moral questions as already settled ; and when they have possessed activity of mind, they have exerted it, not so much in speculative investigation of what ought to be held, as in antiquarian inquiries into what has been held.

" A new school of Christian teachers has sprung up of late years, which neither divides the congregation nor defers to tradition. The Broad Church party, like the High Church party, or, still more, like the Catholic Church, aspires to guide, not a small collection out of the community, but the community itself. It has none of the old pietistic shyness, none of that shrinking from the affairs of the world and society, which is so visible in all sectarian Christianity, and which sometimes assumes the form of an intense nervous antipathy to human beings. It admires the Mediæval Church and Cromwell; it sympathizes with all the attempts which Christianity has made to influence secular government, and to impose its law upon whole communities. But it is unlike the modern Catholic Church, or the old High Church party of England, in not being conservative. By being intensely conservative at a time when society moves with a speed like that of the planet itself through space, the ecclesiastical systems that aspire to government become more hateful to the world than the inoffensive pietistic societies which pretend to nothing of the kind. But the Broad Church party is thoroughly liberal ; it hates obstruction, finality, and every sort of unnatural constraint. It hates, in an especial manner, what may be called ecclesiasticism; so that the clergy of this school are, in a manner, at war with their own order, deplore constantly the weakness and mistakes of 'divines,' and in all disputes appeal to the judgment of the laity. It repudiates the principle of authority in the investigation of truth, and if it abides by some ancient beliefs, and would retain them as the basis of modern order, does so on the ground that they are true, and that they are the best and strongest foundation upon which modern order can be based.

"Before this party, then, there evidently lies a task to which the older parties were not equal. No conservative prejudices, no theological despair, need hinder them from giving the people a Christian morality suited to the age."

While Dr. Muhlenberg never classed himself as a Broad Churchman, and was most decidedly not of that eclectic phase of mind which cultivates the critical habit of thought, and never professed to be a technical scholar with the refined tastes of scholarship, nevertheless he has stood, as has no other leader in the Episcopal Church, for the development both of the personal element and of the established institution. Personality and Institutionalism were the two opposite poles of truth with him. He passed in the days of his own generation as a visionary, a dreamer, a beautiful spirit with Utopian ideas continually before him, but not as one of the practical men of the church's life and thought. To-day the so-called practical men of that period are forgotten, while the practical spirit of Muhlenberg is at the van of the church's life of the present. This chapter has been called "The Growth of Institutionalism through the Genius of his Personality." Let a few added words explain what is meant by this terminology. By Ecclesiastical Institutionalism is meant, in a broad and generic way, the creations of the church system, the methods of work, and the manifold expression of individual faith and character, through the avenues of that order of things which has become established and founded by authority. An institutional method is that method which has become established by church authority, and by the habits of ecclesiastical life in the past, so that it has become the accepted and conventional mode of work, and manner of thought. It is the old channel which needs only the high tide of a strong personality to fill it, so that no dangerous bars or ledges shall prevent a ready access from the haven of the church to the outer sea of the stormy world. It is the fault of many strong personalities that their methods of work must be personal, self - originant, self-willed, and oftentimes wayward. Their individuality, owing in part to the element of intensity, seeks to shatter and destroy the conventional and accepted methods which lesser men rejoice in. Thus it very often happens that a strong personality arrays itself vehemently against the accepted institutions which it finds about it, and so destroys with one hand what it seeks to create with the other. The strong and stormy Berserker-force of the great personality shatters the technique which it finds about it, just as the forceful steam, potent but ill-regulated, destroys the machinery of the conventional engine-room which depends for its success upon schedules, steam-gauges, and safety-valves.

This salient fault of the self-made personality was most carefully avoided by Dr. Muhlenberg. He perceived intuitively the limits both of personality and institutionalism. He knew that the vital force in the church's methods was at times at a low ebb, but he never confounded the lack of force with the mere channel of its manifestation, and in this way he made his personality infuse its power into the old method, and realized our Lord's words when He said, "I am not come to destroy, but to fulfill." Dr. Muhlenberg realized early in life that truth which we all come sooner or later to learn, — that there are vast, ugly, illogical difficulties and brute forces around us, which drive the herd of humanity hither and thither with hungry, cavernous passions; and that it very often happens that our pretty little systems of the past do not reach the hard questions put before our minds for solution. The world of conventional theory is one thing, the world of actual practice is quite another: one is the world of the academy and the college; the other is the world of the knights of labor, where every practical worker in life feels that in some way he must make himself over again for the remaining days of life. It was Dr. Muhlenberg's rare faculty of coördinating the very widely separated elements in his nature, which enabled him in this way to maintain the freshness of his personality, and at the same time to utilize the church's institutional machinery.

The strong and practical men of our professions, business, social, and philanthropic life, too often exhibit that one conspicuous fault of all self-made men, — contempt for the conventional method. The new man and the new plan must have a new method. Here we come across one of the marked limitations of the so-called practical man, and one which Dr. Muhlenberg most happily escaped. The self-made man, the self-educated nature, has no power, in judging merely by its own experience, to comprehend the mental status of those who reach the position upon which they stand by logically accepted methods, and not merely by the by-way method, the hidden, undiscovered path of one's own individuality.

Intuition is good for some natures, — especially for those who have it; but all do not possess this faculty, and therefore the methods of the self-made man should not be heralded as the only method for all sorts and conditions of men.

The power, and yet the weakness, of so-called self-made, self-educated reformers, at times is so plainly evident, that the wise man is he who learns to be afraid of those hidden nooks and by-ways in the markedly individual nature, where the charlatan seeds of error and fallacy grow and flourish. In other words, — and this is the thought to which these opening pages of the present chapter are intended to lead the way, — Dr. Muhlenberg knew the value there is in having a well-trained mind. The philosopher and the practical man were found working in his nature side by side most harmoniously; and in this way he handled, like a successful general upon the field, the very far distant and opposite ends of what but for this might have been a mere poetical and straggling nature. The genius in him submitted most wisely to the discipline of shafts and harness; and thus while he was a theoretical Pegasus, he was at the same time a practical dray-horse. He realized that the trained mind is always a power; that it is the trained mind which does not make haste and is not put to shame; and that it is this which can best lead others, can adapt itself to its limited surroundings, can always take in the situation, and can put itself by the power of sympathy and imagination in the place of others. It was this faculty of the trained or disciplined mind which marked Dr. Muhlenberg's projected endeavors for the welfare of mankind in all his plans for ecclesiastical and social reform. He worked the judgment of others into the raw material of his own schemes; and in this way he avoided waywardness, self-conceit, and the upstart bold- ness of the self-made nature. He kept his per- sonality ever fresh and resolute, ever charged with tonic moral and spiritual resilience; and while he utilized the old conventional methods, he did not despise the familiar pattern of the day of small things. And this is the strong ele- ment in his character, by which he indicated to the church a new field for her hidden activities in that sphere of morality which Professor Seeley has shown was the special mission of the Broad Church party.

His wise and disciplined use of the church's old methods has been of more practical avail than the larger liberty of the Broad Church school of thought, since his schemes have been not in the line of scholastic and analytic criticism, but in that of practical and constructive work.

It has been the development of the church's conventional institutionalism, through the genius of his own fresh and hopeful personality, which has given to Dr. Muhlenberg that conspicuous position of inspired leadership which the Episcopal Church of to-day unmistakably recognizes, and hails with supreme delight.

> " I count life just a stuff
> To try the soul's strength on, — educe the man.
> Who keeps one End in view makes all things serve."
> BROWNING, *In a Balcony.*

Men did not see in Dr. Muhlenberg's lifetime the principle of his life's perspective ; or how it was that, having one end in view, he really did make all things serve. But we see it now, as we look back upon his life ; and that which happened to him, in God's care and oversight, may happen to any one of us if, like Muhlenberg, we make all things serve one end.

The vast benevolent organizations which grew up under Dr. Muhlenberg's hands, although they reached their highest development at a later period in his life than the enterprises reviewed in the foregoing chapters, were no mere afterthought in the scheme of his life's plan. They were involved in the primordial germs of his system ; their prophetic foregleams can be traced in some of his earliest utterances and acts; while the character which he impressed upon them was suffused throughout with heart-warm Evangelical Catholicism. The Evangelical Catholic ideal was too vital and practical a matter to continue always as a mere idea. As all life must find embodiment, so this new force of Christian sentiment was bound to make for itself a corporate outwardness in a body of enduring institutionalism. Like all living bodies, this institutionalism resulting from Dr. Muhlenberg's idea was a growth arising with perfect naturalness, as by manifest destiny, out of the living energy of the idea itself.

The earliest manifestation of organic form which the thought assumed was in the inception of a Church Sisterhood in 1845. At that time there was no organization of the kind in any Protestant communion, either in America or England. He had a clear conviction, even prior to this time, as to the necessity of the womanly element as an agency and influence in any worthy or permanent organization of charity; and the vision of a community of women consecrated to a life of charitable service had floated before him as a working factor in the group of charities which he foresaw growing up around the future Church of the Holy Communion; but he had neither laid any plans nor taken any steps in the matter, when an event occurred which precipitated his action and discovered his skill in improving a favorable opportunity.

This occurrence was nothing less commonplace, nor less to be expected by the true minister of God, than the effectual blessing of God's Holy Spirit upon his words spoken in his name. After listening to a sermon from his lips upon the incident of Jephtha's vow, one of his hearers resolved to consecrate her energies to the undivided service of God in the work of a Sister's life. A very brief interview with Dr. Muhlenberg after the discourse was sufficient to confirm this resolution; and although he had as yet no expectation and no definite plan of entering so soon upon the project of organizing such a band of workers, he nevertheless accepted this as an intimation that God's hour for the task had come, and that he must carry forward what the Spirit of the Lord had thus auspiciously begun. Accordingly, one evening the following winter, in the church, after the dispersion of the congregation from daily service, the first Protestant Sister of the English-speaking world received consecration before the altar at the hands of Dr. Muhlenberg.

To be convinced that this humble germ of institutional life was a plant of the heavenly Father's planting, one needs but to look abroad

and see the vast and varied enterprises of benevolence that are now carried forward by the
devoted activity of Church Sisterhoods in the
United States. The earliest incentive to development in this direction was derived from Dr.
Muhlenberg's successful initiation and management of this first Sisterhood in connection with
the Church of the Holy Communion, and the
administration of St. Luke's Hospital. He
clearly saw that, without the devoted ministry
and consecrated labor of such a band of women,
the successful operation of a great church hospital was more than doubtful. Therefore, in
spite of the prejudice and suspicion incident to
the "Oxford" excitement, he steadily maintained his demand for such an organization of
voluntary nurses, as essential to the hospital
institution, often uttering as an axiom, "No
Sisterhood, no St. Luke's." The utmost tact
and patience were requisite in order to carry the
point in the teeth of suspicious and prejudiced
opposition; and the columns of the "Evangelical Catholic" were used with masterly judgment and effect in softening prejudice and removing unreasoning opposition.

That the character of the organization was an
original conception with him, growing harmoniously and symmetrically out of his Evangelic
Catholic churchmanship, will appear from the

following words of his, introductory to a work entitled " Thoughts on Evangelical Sisterhoods," by the first Sister : —

" At once, then, let it be said, that while we do not underrate the good that is done by such orders as the Sisters of Charity in the Roman communion, we desire to attempt no copying of them among ourselves. They are essentially Roman. To say nothing of their corruptions, and errors of faith, their perpetual vows, their constrained celibacy, their unreserved submission to ecclesiastical rule, their subjection of the conscience to priestly guidance, their onerous rounds of ceremonies and devotions, the whole tenor of their exterior religious life, make them a homogeneous part of the system of that church. They could exist nowhere else. There can be no imitations of them in a Protestant church. ' A Sisterhood ' (the appellation is too good to be given up), as here contended for, is a very simple thing. It is a community of Christian women devoted to works of charity, as the service of their lives, or of a certain portion of them. For the most part they form a household of themselves, that being necessary in order to their mutual sympathy and encouragement, and to their greater unity and efficiency in action. They are held together by identity of purpose, and accordance of will and feeling. Their one bond of union is simply the ' Love of Christ constraining them.' As long as that continues to be a constraining motive, cordially uniting the members, their society will last. In proportion as that languishes and fails, it will decline and dissolve of its own accord. In this respect, as well as in so many others, it differs from any of the religious orders of the Roman Church. To whatever extent these latter are actuated by the genuine life of true charity, yet they have all another and independent life, derived from the system of which they are a component part, and which may be called their ecclesiastical life. Hence they may continue to exist, in virtue of the latter, while the former is no more. Though their proper vitality be gone, the force of the church still acts upon them, impelling them on, and keeping them in action. They may be in a state of moral apostasy; personal piety and virtue may be rare, or be entirely extinct, in them; abuses and corruptions may be multiplying: nevertheless they live and prosper in their own way. They have lost none of their mere ecclesiastical vitality. They retain the imparted energy of 'the church.' Protestantism has no such power. That belongs to a consolidated church. Protestantism possesses not the art of keeping dead things alive. Orders of charity, should they come to pass among us, will be such really and actually as long as they last. They may not last long, but they will be what they profess to be as long as they do last. They will not survive their true and proper existence; they will derive no afterbeing, no perfunctory and mechanical life, from the church. As the spontaneous product of charity, they will thrive just as the spirit of charity continues to be their indwelling spirit. Their corruption will lead to their dissolution. Having only one life, when they are dead they will die. Nothing, then, is to be feared from a truly Evangelical Sisterhood. When it degenerates it will come to an end. It depends for its continuance wholly upon the continuance of the zeal which called it into being. The uniting principle among its members is their common affection for the object which has brought them together, and which, by giving intenseness to their mutual affection as Sisters in Christ, tends to strengthen and confirm their social existence; but there is no constraint from without on the part of the church, not any from within in the form of religious vows, or promises to one another, to insure their perpetuity as a body, or to interfere with their freedom of conscience as individuals. While one in feeling and action, each yet ' stands fast in the liberty wherewith Christ has made us free.' Not that they hold themselves ever ready to adjourn, or that they would be satisfied with an ephemeral existence. Each and all feel that they have entered upon a sacred service, which they are at liberty to quit only at the demand of duty elsewhere. They naturally cherish their union. They look forward to its permanence in themselves, and their successors who may be called thereto. How it may be they do not know. They walk by faith. As they trust their society has come to pass in the gracious ordering of God, so they believe it will be upheld by Him as long as He has work for them to do, and it pleases Him to give them grace to do it. Hand-maidens of the Lord, waiting upon his good pleasure, they are not anxious for the future, content to leave it in his hands."

As regarded any central organization Dr. Muhlenberg said : —

"It is wholly undesirable. We want no such combination, no wide spread of charity, under one head, or church control. Neither, for my part, would I have these associations to be bodies corporate in law, or in any way capable of holding property in their own right. Should they have dwelling-houses, as places of retirement when disabled, or in their old age, these, with moderate endowments, might be held for them by trustees, but nothing further. As simple evangelical associations, not ecclesiastical organizations, the less they have of the means of worldly influence the better. Let this be understood, and any fears or jealousies of a woman - power in the church, which, in fact, would be a priestly power, will have no place. The dread of convents, abbesses, lady superiors, and everything of that sort, will vanish."

The band of Sisters was formally organized under a body of rules, as the Sisterhood of the Church of the Holy Communion, in 1852, and continued during Dr. Muhlenberg's lifetime to render noble service in the various charities of the parish, and in St. Luke's Hospital. And thus the primitive order of deaconesses was, not theoretically but actually, restored to Protestant

Christianity. It was the practical genius and the strong, benevolent personality of Dr. Muhlenberg that effected this, and in so quiet and permanent a manner as hardly served to excite the remark of the Christian public. How many organized and systematic enterprises of charity grew out of his work in the parish of the Holy Communion we have seen in the chapter on "His Type of Churchmanship." His Catholicism was vital, and therefore its concrete embodiment in institutions was instantaneous and inevitable. It was in reference to the rapid spread of this feature of his work, as by a sort of spiritual infection, that the statement has been made that "every movement of spiritual life within the Episcopal Church for the past fifty years may be traced back in some way to Dr. Muhlenberg as its point of departure." [1]

As all genuine growth is silent, so all these noble monuments of his consecrated genius grew up and were carried on in the same quiet, natural, and simple way which so distinguished him in every creation that sprang from his prolific personality. He seemed utterly unconscious that he was doing anything great or remarkable, and went about the initiation of his most astonishing undertakings with the habitual composure and

[1] The late Rev. F. E. Lawrence, Dr. Muhlenberg's successor at the Church of the Holy Communion.

matter-of-course bearing of one engaged in the most ordinary and commonplace occupation.

Thus, as we have already seen at the celebration of the holy communion on St. Luke's Day, 1846, he quietly announced that one half of the offerings for that day would be set apart to be devoted to the founding of a church hospital in the city, to be known as the St. Luke's Hospital, and realized in consequence the paltry sum of $30 with which to inaugurate the history of this now famous and beneficent institution.

Yet the result evinced the wisdom of this method of beginning. On each successive St. Luke's Day the matter was again brought before his people, until their interest began to be excited, and their enthusiasm was aroused, by the church hospital idea. Thus he was able to mould the popular conception of its character, and to hold that conception true to his own idea. At length the proper opportunity for successfully establishing the measure arose, which Dr. Muhlenberg, with his customary sagacity and promptitude, was not slow to embrace. He had done nothing toward realizing his anticipations, except the usual notice on each recurring festival of St. Luke, until the autumn of 1849, when St. Luke's Day was observed by his congregation as an especial thanksgiving for deliverance from the cholera, — only two members having been lost through the plague. The terrible visitation had not only filled the city with grief and terror, but had impressed the public with the great need of better hospital accommodation. It required a scourge to lead the Christian community to perceive this, which Dr. Muhlenberg had long realized with helpless anguish of spirit, and which had compelled him to make his bold move for a church hospital. The congregation and the public generally were in a temper to enter heartily into a thanksgiving service, and to appreciate with cordial favor the importance of the long-projected hospital. The service was worthy of the occasion, with its threefold design of commemoration, thanksgiving, and benevolence. A number of clergymen took part in the service, and the offertory was converted into a general thank offering to be applied to the hospital fund. The result was so encouraging as to justify immediate measures for carrying the project into effect.

Thus was planted, " by the hand of Him who would not let it die," the seed which was destined so soon to grow into one of the most noble institutions of the church in this western world, and to become the model of countless other institutions of like kind and aim to the founding of which the wonderful success of his example first gave the impulse.

Soon after the success of this measure he wrote two lectures, entitled "A Plea for a Church Hospital," and delivered them in different churches throughout the city, to such purpose as to bring the scheme into universal favor. About this time a gift of $10,000 was privately placed in his hand by Mr. Robert B. Minturn toward the new hospital, as a thank offering for a special favor ; and $5,000 were received from an unknown donor through the offertory of the Church of the Holy Communion. In May, 1850, St. Luke's Hospital was incorporated, and the board of managers, with Mr. Robert B. Minturn as president, resolved to solicit the Christian public for the sum of $100,000.

"In pursuance of this," wrote Dr. Muhlenberg, in his sketch of the "History and Progress of St. Luke's," "a meeting of churchmen was held in the Stuyvesant Institute, at which, after addresses by several of the clergy, of different schools or parties, but one in the charity which stills even theological polemics, committees of collection were appointed, and the work was put fairly afloat."

The desired amount was secured much sooner and with much less difficulty than was usual in those days with charitable solicitations; but the last $5,000, given expressly to complete the wished-for sum, was coupled with the condition

that $50,000 more should be raised, which some-
what delayed the completion of the fund, but
the entire amount of $150,000 in subscriptions
was in due time realized. Dr. Muhlenberg
having meanwhile, in a manner peculiar to himself, mastered the whole inevitable array of difficulties and debates about a site for the new
hospital building, the corner-stone was laid May
6, 1854, by Bishop Wainwright. His plan in
reference to the design of the building, "to provide rooms for the good women, the Sisters, who,
under the pastor and superintendent, it was tac-
itly understood, were to have charge of the sick,"
was unanimously opposed and forbidden by the
board on its first mention.

This unforeseen opposition came near wreck-
ing Dr. Muhlenberg's most cherished plan of an
agency for the Christian economy of the proposed hospital, without which he clearly foresaw
that the results of the institution in relation to
the kingdom of God, as well as its humanitarian
success, could never be what he designed that
they should be. We who are familiar with the
work of the Protestant sisterhoods among the
charitable agencies of all our large cities cannot
readily understand the deep-seated prejudice
and aversion with which the very name was regarded in the days when the only sisterhood in
the land was that which Dr. Muhlenberg had

brought into being in connection with the work
of his own parish. The prejudice was an element in the public opinion of the time which
the hospital board did not dare disregard, although personally they were not affected by it.
By judicious delays, however, and some minor
concessions, the fears of "Puseyite sisters" and
"Protestant nuns" were so far allayed or ban-
ished from the public mind that by the time the
hospital was opened they were admitted to their
true place and function in its domestic administration.

After six months passed abroad in studying
the great hospitals of London and Paris, Dr.
Muhlenberg returned, in the autumn of 1855,
to superintend the building of St. Luke's. He
did not borrow his design of the building, however, from any European institution. That was
determined upon before going abroad. The
architect, Mr. J. W. Rich, was directed to start
with that which had been the design of Dr.
Muhlenberg from the beginning, namely, a central chapel immediately communicating with the
wards. Corridors running lengthwise outside
the wards, and connected with the chapel, made
the latter, with its ample windows, a reservoir
of fresh air, which permeated the entire building by means of the double stairways, and could
be admitted at will into the wards. The chapel

and its Christian offices were the central features of Dr. Muhlenberg's conception of the hospital building and administration. He never lost sight of its foundation idea and distinctive character as a church institution. Catholic brotherhood was the dominant idea in this "Hospital Church," — his favorite name for it, — as in all his other conceptions. The hospital wards, three hundred feet long, radiating from the chapel, he used to call the "long-drawn aisles of his cathedral." His grand voice and distinct articulation carried every word of the service through the open doors to the remotest occupant in the wards, and by means of their successive inmates he claimed to have preached the gospel, in the aggregate, to many more souls than did the rectors of the largest city churches. The chapel was completed and opened for divine worship one year before the opening of the hospital proper, — that is, on Ascension Day, 1857. Meanwhile subscriptions had been opened for an addition of another $100,000 to the building fund, which was raised after some delays, and the whole was completed and formally opened at the festival of the Ascension, May 13, 1858. Dr. Muhlenberg, with characteristic energy, secured the means to furnish the wards, and they were speedily filled with patients, under the care of the Sisterhood.

There were no funds in existence as yet with which to meet the running expenses of the hospital, but Dr. Muhlenberg's simple faith was an inexhaustible capital in itself, which made suspension or failure impossible. The proposition to postpone the opening of the hospital until such a fund could be provided met with an emphatic refusal upon his part. He knew that the fountains of living charity in the community would be quickened and enlarged by means of this waiting, trusting attitude on the part of the hospital authorities, and he was not disappointed. No sooner was it understood that Dr. Muhlenberg himself had, by agreement with the managers, assumed all responsibility as to household expenses for the first three years, than plentiful donations began to pour in from that large part of the Christian public interested in the success of the institution. Hospital associations were formed, at Dr. Muhlenberg's instigation, among the young men of the different city parishes, who charged themselves with the duty of searching out, bringing to the hospital, and maintaining while there, the sick and destitute who came under their observation; the members also visiting the beneficiaries while in the hospital, providing decent Christian burial in case of death, and interesting themselves to set them on their way again in life if they recovered.

From the first, Dr. Muhlenberg made the Hospital what the Institute and College had been in years gone by, — a Christian family, in the character of its association and the quality of its ministries. He was, at the date of its opening, still rector of the Parish of the Holy Communion, but it was not his manner to superintend such an enterprise until it was ready to be launched on its proper work, and then commit its destiny to other hands. He never lost sight of the guiding principle in all his undertakings, that a controlling and moulding personality is the mainspring always in any institution. As he had merged his life with that of his boys in the Institute, in order to insure its development into the character which he had conceived for it, so now no other thought entered his mind than that he, as resident pastor and superintendent, must be the formative and animating spirit of St. Luke's, in order to determine its proper administration as a Christian hospital; and in 1859 he relinquished all direct responsibility for the Parish of the Holy Communion, and devoted himself to the management and pastoral duties of St. Luke's. What he was to St. Luke's for the first twenty years of its history, as pastor and executive head, in the new system of nursing which he introduced, with the element of personal interest, and intelligent, conscientious, responsible care as its leading feature; in the personal solicitude with which he ministered to the spiritual necessities of the stricken inmates; in the atmosphere of home-like cheer and peace and comfort which pervaded the house as the effect of his benignant presence; in the sacred offices of religion which he performed with solemnizing, comforting, and elevating results, — these things cannot be written down. "Pastoral," or "practical" theology, like "pedagogics" so called, is not a science to be acquired and dispensed by rule. The cure of souls is an art, and in this, as in all art, the personal element dominates everything; and a personality is a thing which, in its full flavor and effect, can never be communicated on paper. The ministry was to Dr. Muhlenberg emphatically, above everything else, the *cure* of souls.

St. Johnland was the most characteristic of all Dr. Muhlenberg's public undertakings. It embodied more of his personality in its spirit and aims than any other of his benevolent plans, and more nearly expressed the Christly temper of his heart. Perhaps the distance by which his life and faith, in their nearness to Jesus of Nazareth, were removed from the covetous heart of an unbelieving generation, may be indicated by the significant fact that, notwithstanding its instant and permanent success as an industrial

community established upon principles of genuinely Christian socialism, it has had no imi-
tators. It is the one type of institutionalism,
growing out of his personality, which the temper of the time has not suffered to spread.

Perhaps this may be owing to the fact that
much of our benevolent work in the present age
is done by committees, and not by individuals.
Committees, like corporations, often have no
souls, whereas God, when He would speak to the
world, has always spoken by prophets, and not
by committees.

In all these years since Dr. Muhlenberg founded this unique society, as a living exemplifica-
tion of the principles of Christ in the social life,
the Christian public have been eagerly combat-
ing or apologizing for abstract theories of social
reorganization, which, if left unnoticed, would
die of themselves; the priest and the Levite
have still gone down, according to their wont,
from Jerusalem to Jericho, and, after looking
on the festering sores of the social body, suffering and wounded by humanity's conventional
thieves, have passed by on the other side, absorbed in wise discourse about the methods of
preventing the self-same thieves from plying
their trade; but, since Dr. Muhlenberg, no
good Samaritan has so far denied himself the
innate delight which the world of theory seems

to afford, as to manifest any skill or enthusiasm in the very practical matter of providing an inn where the native energies of the sufferer may have opportunity to rally.

This precisely was the effort and aim of Dr. Muhlenberg in the St. Johnland venture. He purchased about six hundred acres of land on the north side of Long Island, combining all the natural advantages essential to such an experiment. Upon this tract he founded a village, composed, for the most part, of single cottages. The purpose of this community life he has explained at length in words which once read like prophecy and are now a matter of every day history.

This latest venture of St. Johnland, as he himself has described it with his own directness, was the modest and spiritual contribution of this man of action towards the solution of the social problems of the age, with which the most active minds have been grappling for so long, with little or no practical and enduring result. The comprehensive and acute thinker, who undertakes to master all the factors in the problem of the inequalities of wealth distribution, will sooner or later reach the conviction of his incapacity to grasp and hold in due relation and perspective the vast and varied elemental forces involved ; and he will more and more be disposed to doubt his right to have or to express decided opinions on the subject. Dr. Muhlenberg persistently declined to attempt any "solution" at all. He had no theory of social reorganization which was to operate as a panacea for all existing evils. He saw with bitter sorrow the grievous ills of the present order, and he portrayed them in words of vivid and powerful eloquence;[1] and he did what in him lay, in the way of practical effort, towards social amelioration without previously announcing any theory.

In all this he was but showing most unmistakably that growth and development of the spiritual nature within him which always, through the sheer force of its divine and tonic power, conquers the material side of life, and solves the hard problems of the social world with that penetrating light and fire which come from the depth of being where God is, the place which old Jacob Boehme used to call the "fire-world of the divine abyss."

A fair analysis of Dr. Muhlenberg's work and achievements in this field reveals, however, these underlying principles, — that the end of human existence and social order is the production of a perfect type of individual and corporate character; that character is a growth,

---

[1] *Vide, e. g.*, the concluding paragraphs of the "Retro-Prospectus," *Evangelical Catholic Papers*, First Series.

a continuous evolution, the result of an educational process in which the interaction of individual and corporate energies is the indispensable factor. He regarded the family as the true social unit, or rather as in a sense the nest-idea of the social organism, to mould and determine the development of individual character. Hence his effort toward social amelioration contemplated the elevation and education of families as the chief result of its action. It is sufficient to say that, if the New Testament idea of social order and progress be the true one, then he was right in this ; if that be mistaken and wrong, then his effort was unmeaning and worthless. At any rate he never surrendered the organic conception of Christianity to the absorbing demands of an over-wrought individualism.

A moderate rent was charged for the cottages at St. Johnland, less than the amount extorted for half the space in wretched dens of the city, which was to be devoted to the running expenses of the enterprise, — repairs, salary of agent, transportation, etc., no one being allowed, by the act of incorporation, to realize any profit from this source. He held that this was necessary in any scheme for teaching the poor to help themselves. Free cottages would be subversive of independence, and result in pauperization. The project had nothing of the eleemosynary or reformatory character in its main idea. It was a socialistic community, founded upon the purest and most Catholic Christian principles. There were many difficulties in the way of this latest venture of Christian socialism, as there has always hung a cloud and shadow over similar enterprises, from the days of Ananias and Sapphira in the early Apostolic Church to the latest experiments of the Brook Farm and the Anti-poverty Society; but one by one, at least during the lifetime of Dr. Muhlenberg, or after his death, these difficulties disappeared, just as the congealed ice in some dangerous mountain pass does not argue with the rising sun, but simply vanishes away. To be strictly honest, however, it must be confessed that until recently St. Johnland has been the least successful of all Dr. Muhlenberg's ventures of faith. But his many friends believed thoroughly in the future of this work; and that eminent Christian philosopher and preacher, the late Dr. Edward Washburn, gave direction that his body should rest by the side of his friend in the quiet shadows of St. Johnland's village church, and there these two companions, who were lovely and pleasant in their lives, in their death are not divided.

The following description of St. Johnland as it is at present is taken from the last annual report of the institution for the year 1888:—

The Church Industrial Community of St. John-land is situated on the north shore of Long Island, forty-five miles from New York city. It was founded in 1866 by the Rev. Dr. Muhlenberg, as a home for aged men, and young children of both sexes, especially cripples. In 1870 "The Society of St. Johnland" was incorporated, under whose control the work has been since carried on. It is reached by the Port Jefferson branch of the Long Island Railroad from Long Island City, by two trains each way daily.

The St. Johnland domain consists of five hundred and thirty-five acres, with a frontage of nearly a mile and a half on Long Island Sound. About two hundred acres are under cultivation. The estate is beautifully diversified with hill and dale. The village is located on the southern slope of a high bluff which here skirts the Sound. There are over thirty buildings, and a population varying from two hundred to two hundred and fifty.

Just back of the village is a magnificent grove of old oak and chestnut trees, which, from time immemorial, was the favorite picnic ground for the surrounding neighborhood. A strong stairway leads to the foot of the bluff, near the mouth of a little creek, where the children bathe daily during the season.

The woods are filled with wild fruits and nuts in season ; and as a large part of the domain is covered with timber, there is ample room for young and old to exercise their activities.

The community is a little world in itself. There

is a very pretty church, where daily services are held ; a neat school-house, accommodating ninety children ; a library with a good supply of books ; a store, where the supplies are bought at wholesale, and distributed to the different homes ; a bakery, where white and brown bread are baked every day ; a tailor shop, where a tailor, with several apprentices, makes clothing for the beneficiaries ; a cobbler's shop, where an old man is kept busy in repairing the ravages of work and play upon the children's shoes ; a laundry, where all the washing is done ; a carpenter's shop ; a blacksmith's shop ; a garden, where a full supply of vegetables is raised ; and a farm and dairy.

The principal buildings of St. Johnland at this time are as follows : —

THE CHURCH OF THE TESTIMONY OF JESUS. — In the midst of the settlement, on rising ground, it stands, a goodly rural sanctuary, seventy feet long and sixty feet wide across the transepts. It was built in 1869, the sole gift of Mr. Adam Norrie. His daughter, Miss Julia Norrie, furnished the bell, and a beautiful communion service of silver. An elegant marble font was given by Mrs. S. Weir Roosevelt. Through the late Mr. Hilborne L. Roosevelt, several gentlemen united in the gift of a pipe organ.

In the belfry tower has since been placed the " Town Clock," which strikes the hours. The church will seat about three hundred. Short services are held daily in the morning and evening, and on Sundays the usual Morning and Evening Services of the Church.

St. John's Inn, or the Home for Old Men. — This house was built in 1869 by Mr. John David Wolfe, who supplied the entire cost. It is the largest structure in the village, and is admirably adapted to its use. It consists of a centre building forty-five by seventy feet, with wings on either side, each thirty by thirty-five, and connected with the centre building by inclosed corridors, — the whole presenting a handsome front of one hundred and fifty feet. The main building contains the general refectory, kitchen, linen room, and rooms for the Matron and several girls. The wings, known respectively as the East and West Wings, are the quarters for the old men. They are two stories high, the upper floor being reached by a broad, easy staircase. Each floor consists of a sitting-room extending from front to rear, with a row of alcoves on each side. These alcoves are separated from each other by a board partition, and from the sitting-room by heavy curtains. Each alcove is furnished with a bed, bureau, washstand, etc., and is lighted by a large window. The sitting-rooms are well lighted and ventilated, and comfortably heated. A few steps away is the church, while the library is at easy distance.

The Spencer and Wolfe Home. — This was the first of the Children's Homes at St. Johnland. It was the gift of Mrs. C. L. Spencer and Miss Catharine Wolfe. One thousand dollars was contributed by Mrs. Wyman towards the furnishing of the house.

It is a substantial building of fifty by thirty feet, with a wing of almost the same dimensions on the western and a smaller wing on the eastern end. The dining-room is at the left on entering the hall. To the right is a neat little parlor. Above the dining-room is a large dormitory. In the western extension are the play-room, used when the weather is inclement, a large dormitory, and several small rooms. In the eastern extension are the kitchen and pantry. This home will accommodate thirty-six girls.

THE FABBRI HOME. — This was the first cottage built in St. Johnland, and was intended to accommodate two families. Owing to the crowded condition of the Boys' House it became necessary to adapt it to the uses of the large boys, which was done in 1883, Mr. Egisto P. Fabbri, the original donor of the cottage, supplying the means for its enlargement.

It is three stories high, with a story and a half addition on the western end. Originally it was a long, low building, but now, though plain, is considered as one of the neatest buildings on the grounds. On the lower floor are rooms for the Matron and her assistant, a large social room, and lavatories. The second and third floors are used as dormitories, the second floor having six alcoves divided by curtains. There are twenty-two beds in this home.

THE BOYS' HOUSE, OR JOHNNY'S MEMORIAL. — This home for boys was built by a niece of Dr. Muhlenberg's, Mrs. W. E. Chisolm, in memory of her eldest son, John Rogers Chisolm, who was taken away very unexpectedly in his tenth year.

The house is a substantial edifice of two stories and a high basement. Its dimensions are thirty by sixty feet. The basement contains the kitchen and dining-room, where all the boys are fed. The first story has the play-room, sitting-room, and rooms for the Matron and others. The upper floor is divided into two large dormitories, well ventilated by the dormer windows which give a picturesque appearance to the roof. Thirty-six of the smaller boys live in this house.

THE LIBRARY AND VILLAGE HALL. — This is a substantial structure, at the eastern extremity of the village. It is thirty feet front, by forty deep, two stories high, with a good brick basement, and a tower rising from the portico.

The upper room is the Library, with more than two thousand volumes, among them the libraries of Dr. Muhlenberg, and that of his friend, Rev. Dr. Crusé, sometime librarian of the General Theological Seminary.

The lower floor is the Village Hall, where, during the winter season, entertainments of various kinds are given at frequent intervals. A platform neatly carpeted is at one end, with a convenient dressing-room formed by papered screens. A handsome upright Weber piano is near the platform, and the room is neatly seated. It will accommodate two hundred persons, and is a marked feature in our social life.

THE SUNBEAM COTTAGE. — In point of architecture, this is the gem of the village. It is a very commodious and substantial structure built in the Queen Anne style, and is well equipped in every respect. The purpose for which this house is intended is expressed in a Memorial Tablet placed over the beautiful carved mantel in the hall : " For the education and training of orphan girls, this house is erected by Mr. and Mrs. Cornelius Vanderbilt, A. D. 1881, in memory of their eldest daughter, who entered into life eternal Oct. 31, 1873."

A wide hall runs entirely through the house, at the north end of which is a broad, winding staircase with stained glass windows, designed by La Farge, rising with the steps. On each of these windows is a quaint proverb.

The first floor contains a kitchen, dining-room, sitting-room, and play-room. The second floor has two large dormitories, Matron's room, infirmary, bathroom, and lavatories. The third floor contains several rooms for the larger girls, and a large rainy-day play-room. This cottage has recently been repaired both within and without, and everything put in the most complete repair.

The whole house is so bright and sunny that it well deserves the name of Sunbeam Cottage.

THE OFFICE AND INDUSTRIAL SCHOOL are in the building formerly used as a printing office. The Office is in the eastern end of the lower floor, while the west end has been fitted as a school-room for primary and industrial work.

The Tailor Shop and dormitories for employees occupy the upper part of the building ; these dormitories at present are occupied by old men for whom there is no accommodation at the Inn.

THE SCHOOL-HOUSE. — This was built in 1881, and was the last benefaction to us of Mr. Adam Norrie, whose gifts were manifold, and who was one of the earliest friends of St. Johnland. His daughter, Miss Julia Norrie, united in the gift. The School-house is located at the extreme western end of the main row of buildings. It is a neat structure of tasteful architecture.

The school-room is divided through the centre by rolling doors, thus making two apartments, which are used as the Boys' and Girls' Schools.

The rooms are well lighted and ventilated, and are fitted with comfortable desks, blackboards, and maps, and whatever is needed for successful teaching.

THE MANSION. — This is the original homestead of the farm, but was enlarged by Dr. Muhlenberg. It was his home whenever he visited St. Johnland, and was occupied by Sister Anne during her charge of the place. It is now the residence of the Super-intendent and his family.

THE CEMETERY. — On a beautiful knoll back of the Inn, surrounded by a neat rustic fence, is the Cemetery, in which are the graves of Dr. Muhlenberg and Dr. Washburn.

There has always been a secret, fatal flaw in all schemes of socialism and Christian coöper-ation, from the days of the Apostles to the pres-ent time. All colonization societies which have been planted on the moral basis have been branded with the unerring mark of failure, and not yet has the keen political economist been able to detect this secret cause of discord and

confusion in the many plans of benevolent co-
operation which adorn the pages of history.

This, however, must at least be said in defense
of this latest projected scheme of Dr. Muhlenberg's, that the greater prophets of sacred history
have always been followed by the minor prophets,
who have supplemented the work of their prede-
cessors, as Elisha came after Elijah, and Paul,
who called himself the least of the Apostles, followed after the short but effective ministry of
the young Stephen, who, we are told, impressed
his age as one who was "full of faith and
power." Perhaps the boy is now at school, or
the youth in college, who will even yet develop
and make vital in the coming generation this
latest dream of the aged Muhlenberg.

In "The Church of To-day," November 7,
1889, is printed the following account of St.
Johnland : —

"This institution, founded by Dr. Muhlenberg,
was probably never more prosperous than now, and
both within and without never has presented a finer
appearance. Since the Rev. Mr. Gassner was appointed superintendent, some three years ago, he has
not only kept the institution within its income, but
without increased expenses has year by year greatly
improved the grounds, so that they were never before
anything like so attractive. Some forty aged men
are cared for in 'St. John's Inn,' one of whom

celebrated his eightieth birthday the past week by walking to Northport and back again, a distance of fourteen miles. In other cottages some sixty girls and forty-five boys are cared for, and also taught by efficient teachers. The healthy and neat appearance of the children could scarcely be improved. In the Sunbeam Cottage, built and supported by Mr. and Mrs. Cornelius Vanderbilt as a memorial of a daughter, there are twenty of the girls, ranging from five to fifteen years of age. On Sundays the chapel is nearly filled with the inmates of the cottages, old and young, the music being well rendered by a large double choir of young girls. The children have three excellent teachers, and the school has all the advantages of common-school education."

Concerning the present success of St. Johnland the Rev. George S. Gassner, superintendent and pastor of St. Johnland, writes as follows : —

"NEW YORK, *November* 19, 1889.

. . . "The fundamental idea of St. Johnland as projected by Dr. Muhlenberg — a collection of homes for industrial workers — has not been found practicable simply owing to the fact that the poor will not leave the city. As a home for old men and children, it is probably unsurpassed. We are endeavoring to keep alive the traditions of the place as left by its illustrious founder."

The Rev. Dr. E. Winchester Donald, one of the trustees of St. Johnland, and vice-president of the board, also gives his opinion of the

working success of this colony in the following
words : —

"NEW YORK, *November* 19, 1889.

. . . "St. Johnland is in better shape than it has
been for a dozen or more years, — out of debt and
with an increased endowment. Indeed, it is now a
great success."

To say that the work at St. Johnland has not
been such a success as the other institutions from
this creative mind, is but to admit that those
who have carried it on have felt the loss of
its creator's inspiration. Human nature is strong
in many differing ways, — at many opposite
angles of being, — and not in the same direction.
Where one man may be strong, another may be
weak ; and that which many movements need
is that which Israel wanted when Moses died, —
a Joshua to lead the people in to the promised
land of their inheritance. Besides this, St. Johnland was wanting in the element of adaptiveness
to the times and to human nature's needs. It
was necessarily lacking in the essential elements
of reproductiveness. It was a specimen, not a
genus, and was another experiment upon an
always doubtful field. St. Luke's Hospital, on
the other hand, was always an assured success,
simply because it was within the field of the
ever-present practical. It belonged not to the
specimen, but to the *genus* category.

In addition to this it must be added that the weak point in Dr. Muhlenberg's " Retro-Prospectus," like that in Edward Bellamy's remarkable work of to-day, "Looking Backward," as in all backward visions of the present from the standpoint of the hypothetical future, consists in the fact that the seer who looks backward always forgets that he must create an imaginary future, which never can be like the real future, because he has not and can never have the material out of which the scaffolding for building the future can be made.

We project into the future imaginary conditions, conceived out of our present state of life. But the future comes always with unknown and unfamiliar conditions, so that it always beggars and belittles our outlook.

But however this may be, things which were easy to Dr. Muhlenberg seemed difficult if not impossible to others. For the call of God reached his rich nature intuitively, and the nature replied with a lavish wealth of expression, which in poetry might have been a poem, or in sculpture might have proved a carving, or in music a sonata; but which, since the field of its development was religion, asserted itself in the beautiful form of a divine and practical piety.

It is impossible to convey any adequate impression of the atmosphere of joyous, radiant, religious life with which the spiritual genius of Dr. Muhlenberg enveloped and pervaded the nascent community of St. Johnland. Perhaps the nearest approach to such an impression will be obtained by a perusal of his " Retro-Prospectus," [1] a sprightly and earnest pamphlet by means of which he initiated the St. Johnland movement. The whole character of its religious life is that of genuine spontaneity, of reverent devotion, and warm, catholic brotherhood.

The one psalm of praise and thanksgiving which might well have been chanted at the opening of St. Johnland was the "Exurgat Deus" of the 68th Psalm, — that triumphant pæan of jubilant Israel : —

" Let God arise, and let his enemies be scattered : let them also that hate Him flee before Him. O sing unto God, and sing praises unto his name. He is a father of the fatherless, and defendeth the cause of the widows ; even God in his holy habitation. He is the God that maketh men to be of one mind in an house, and bringeth the prisoners out of captivity.

O God, when thou wentest forth before the people, when thou wentest through the wilderness, the earth shook and the heavens dropped at the presence of God, who is the God of Israel. Thou, O God, *sentest* a gracious rain upon thine inheritance, and refreshedst it when it was weary. Thy congregation shall

---

[1] *Evangelical Catholic Papers*, First Series.

dwell therein, for thou of thy goodness hast **prepared**
a place for the poor."

At the founding of the Church of the Testimony he drew up a declaration, in which the
following rights and privileges were reserved,
namely, "the liberty of conscience," "the liberty of prayer," and "the liberty of ministerial fellowship." He also prepared a "Directory for Worship," to be used by this church,
which is a monument of his saintly Johannean
mind. It provides for considerable liberty of
omission in the use of the various offices of the
Book of Common Prayer, and for a very exten-
sive liberty of substitution or alteration from
the habitual use. Whoever wishes to obtain a
glimpse of the wide range of Dr. Muhlenberg's
liturgical inspiration, and the marked versatil-
ity of his devotional genius, must get it by the
study of this, the least appreciated and most ele-
vated of his works. And whoever wishes to find
an actual illustration of Evangelical Catholic
worship must find it in that of the St. Johnland "Church of the Testimony of Jesus."

There are times in life when, in order to go
forward wisely and with the divine assurance of
strength, we must go back to the ideal standard
of the past, which in our busy haste we have
passed by in contemptuous neglect. There are
certain critical moments in the life of the church

when all the finger-boards on the upward journey point in the same direction. The Spirit
of God himself, the divine warner of all souls,
and the intuitions of the baffled and perplexed
heart of man alike point in the same direction,
and say to us in our moments of religious and
moral prostration, Go back, go back, and take
up once again the pattern shown to you in the
mount of the ideal.

And to-day the practical workers and thinkers
in the church are going back to the ideal standards of Muhlenberg, which have been covered
with the dust of thirty years of unbelief and distrust.

But the aged saint did not live long to see the
assured success of this latest child of his benevolent creating.

On the 12th day of April, 1879, a solemn
funeral train, with Bishop Kerfoot among its
numbers, followed the mortal remains of this
eminent saint of God from the city of his late
labors to their earthly resting place, this child
of his old age, his beloved St. Johnland. There
was just light enough, on arriving, to descry the
sobbing groups issuing from the different houses.
All followed the funeral train into the church,
dimly lighted at the chancel, where the remains
were reverently placed, and from that moment
faithfully guarded by relays of young male com-

municants, both throughout the night and until the hour of burial next day. The little sanctuary was thronged, making deep, solemn shadows in the unlighted aisle. It was impossible to separate without united prayer. The bishop led in an improvised service, not a mournful one, but looking upwards, whither the sainted father had gone, lifting the thoughts of those true mourners from the sad mortality before their eyes to the unspeakable joy of his beatified soul in Paradise.

On the afternoon of the following day, upon the summit of the knoll overlooking the quiet valley toward which his heart had gone out so often in loving desires and heavenly benediction, in the spot which he himself had indicated as his last resting place, the dust of "everybody's father," the St. John of the American church, was committed to the earth.

There let us leave him, amid the quiet success and abounding blessing of this final venture of his faith, with its hitherto unheeded appeal to the "beneficent powers and processes of the Unseen Time."

NOTE. — The Rev. William Allan Fair, in the Bassa District of the West African Mission, has very kindly forwarded the inclosed letter from Africa to the compiler of the present volume.

The letter is valuable, coming as it does unsought,

and as showing the interest which Dr. Muhlenberg felt, though absent, in his children at St. Johnland, where Mr. Fair was at that time a teacher.

" *To Mr. William Fair, St. Johnland, L. I., New York, U. S. A.*

"Brussels, *August* 4, 1872.

"My dear Mr. Fair:

"I send you a few words for the good folk at St. Johnland. Remember me affectionately to Mr. Gordon, — Edward, — and to our dear housekeeper, Miss Russell.

"Hoping you are all well, —

"W. A. M.

"Get one of the older boys to write me a letter, signed by the others."

"Brussels, *Sunday, August* 4.

"My dear Children of St. Johnland, Old and Young:

"I have just been at church, where we had the service of the Prayer Book by an English clergyman, who gave us no sermon; so, instead of listening to one myself, I will write a short one to you, — not a sermon, however, but a few words of remembrance for Mr. Fair to read to you in church.

"I need not tell you how often I have you all in my thoughts, — hoping that, could I hear of you, I would learn nothing to make me sad. I trust that all are going on cheerfully and harmoniously with their several duties; I am sure that such is the case with those who are in charge of the different departments of the work at St. Johnland, and I please myself with believing that you, my younger friends, are also doing your parts, day by day, with a good conscience; especially you, my dear boys, I hope, are dutiful and obedient, keeping the rules, giving Mr. Gordon and Mr. —— no trouble, so that they and Mr. Fair will have nothing bad to tell me of any of you.

"Let me remind you of what I have so often said to you about your good behavior, especially on Sundays. Be thankful that God has placed you where his holy day is kept, so different from here, where I am writing. Brussels is a small Paris. Business is going on like any other day; shops are all open; going to and from church I saw only one or two shut; the after part of the day is given up to gayety and amusement, theatres, concerts, etc. You know that in New York many want the same kind of Sunday, but I hope God will preserve us from it; and that you will do what you can, in your day and generation, towards saving the land from losing the blessing of a Christian Sabbath. . . . I hope to do more good among you when it pleases God to bring us together again.

"Pray for us, as we do continually for you in our devotions, never forgetting St. Johnland.

"Your loving pastor,

"W. A MUHLENBERG."

THE AFTER–GLOW OF HIS IN-
FLUENCE.

"Unenfeebled will I bring my spirit down to life's closing period ; never shall the genial courage of life desert me ; what gladdens me now shall gladden me ever. My imagination shall continue lively and my will unbroken, and nothing shall force from my hand the magic key which opens the mysterious gates of the upper world ; and the fire of love within me shall never be extinguished. I will not look upon the dreaded weakness of age ; I pledge myself to supreme contempt of every toil which does not concern the true end of my existence ; and I vow to remain forever young. . . . The spirit which impels men forward shall never fail me, and the longing which is never satisfied with what has been, but ever goes forth to meet the new, shall still be mine. The glory I shall seek is to know that my aim is infinite, and yet never to pause in my course. . . .

"I shall never think myself old till my work is done, and that work will not be done while I know and will what I ought. . . . To the end of life I am determined to grow stronger and livelier by every act, and more vital through every self-improvement. . . . When the light of my eyes shall fade, and the gray hairs shall sprinkle my blonde locks, my spirit shall still smile." — SCHLEIERMACHER.

> "Skillful alike with tongue and pen,
> He preached to all men everywhere
> The Gospel of the Golden Rule,
> The new commandment given to men.
> With reverent feet the earth he trod,
> Nor banished nature from his plan,
> But studied still, with deep research,
> To build the universal church,
> Lofty as is the love of God,
> And ample as the wants of man."
>
> LONGFELLOW, *Tales of a Wayside Inn.*

CHAPTER VI.

THE AFTER-GLOW OF HIS INFLUENCE.

HAVING in the previous chapters of this book told the story of Dr. Muhlenberg's life, in this closing chapter it is reserved to paint the character with those definite colors which we find at the sunset hour, — a pleasure which has been forborne in all that has gone before, in order that the character might have full justice at the end. There are two facts which come home to us all in life, as we find ourselves growing further away from the freshness of our youth, with a sense of their persistent power. One of these facts is the realization of our bygone moments of inspiration; the other fact is the realization of new difficulties in life, for which we find no adequate solution.

In all the old days, we used to carry fire and conviction enough for the problems which came before us. Now, we too often find that either the new problems are too much for us, or that there is some leak or waste in the moral system by which the strength needed for the new trial or emergency has departed, and we realize the truthfulness of the words of Arthur Hugh Clough when he wrote : —

> "We are most hopeless who had once most hope,
>   And most beliefless who had once believed."

This prostration of the moral nature was something which seemed to be utterly unknown to Dr. Muhlenberg. He was ever fresh, with a resilience and a recuperative energy which reminds one of the youth of the immortals.

The secret of this innate freshness is explained by a fact of philosophy found in a certain sermon of F. W. Robertson, in which he says : —

> "Strength of character consists of two things, — power of will, and power of self-restraint. It requires, therefore, two things for its existence, — strong feelings and strong command over them. To judge of a man truly, you must measure his strength by the power of the feelings he subdues, not by the power of those that subdue him, and hence composure is very often the highest result of strength."

This truth is put in another form by George Eliot in her story of "Janet's Repentance," where we come across these words : " The early heroes of God's making know one or two of these deep spiritual truths, which are only to be won by long wrestling with their own sins and their own sorrows. They have recognized faith and strength so far as they have done genuine work ;

but the rest is often dry theory, blank prejudice, and vague hearsay." It was the genuine work done in his lifetime which gave this man his peace and power at the end of his days. The first revelation of all influence in character is generally the period of early impulse. To most of us, this is the period of childhood and youth and early idealism. It is the period of tender sentiment and of flowering possibilities. But with this leader of religious thought, this early impulse apparently lasted throughout the entire life, and was never followed by any lack of moral perspective. It was sustained throughout a long life in which there never seemed to be the loss of this faculty ; and though at times he felt most keenly the criticism of those who could not understand him, and who in consequence withdrew from him their sympathy, the habitude of calm and holy living crowned his life all the way through to its close.

It is of the after-glow of Dr. Muhlenberg's influence that we are to treat in the present chapter. Have any of the readers of this book ever analyzed the constituent elements which help to form that phenomenon in nature which we call an after-glow ?

From the rocky bluffs of the Narragansett shore across the waters which form the Mediterranean climate of our own Atlantic coast, warmed by the Gulf Stream current, and fanned by the soft breezes, which, according to the Indian legend, are the whisperings of the good spirits from the south, on many a September evening the lingering visitor may ponder over the wonderful revelation of nature's after-glow, when the sun has gone down, and when the heavens seem on fire.

A departing light, a wide field for reflection, and an emanation which seems as if it were something higher than a mere material effect, are the three definite elements which make an after-glow in nature. The heavens are bright with the light of the departing sun; the rocks and trees and the surf upon the shore are purple and golden with the refracted beams; and across the vast expanse of sky and sea a molten emanation seems to typify the influence and the power of the orb of light, which because it has departed is seen in its effects rather than in itself. It is an after-glow, we say, and it is the after-glow of the sun's influence.

It is concerning the influence of Dr. Muhlenberg after his life has been lived which is the subject of this closing chapter. His life was a definite light; that light worked outwards upon a definite field, and the emanation from this life has a positive and definite influence to-day. It is like the auroral light in the heavens, tell-

ing of a far-off pole of magnetic power; it is
like the after-glow of the sun when the sun has
gone down, but when the heavens seem to be
ablaze with light: it is the after-glow of Muhlenberg's strong and saintly character.

There are other names in the annals of the
Episcopal Church of America which have a more
commanding sound on the lesser pages of local
and technical history than that of our poet and
philanthropist. Bishop White with his simple
purity and power, Bishop Alonzo Potter with his
wide-hearted churchmanship, Bishop McIlvaine
with his commanding social influence, or Bishop
Hobart with his aggressive work for Episcopal
technique, might well be chosen as representative
leaders of the church in America. But there
was a rounded perfection about these names
which limited their influence to that side of the
church's life of which they were the representatives. They were so logical in those lesser matters, for which their names have become the
synonyms, that they were not logical enough for
the whole church, which on its many sides seems
illogical, and should therefore be represented in
its totality by one who in his day and generation
was deemed an illogical philanthropist, concerning whom the verdict of Joseph's brethren was
given, "We will see what will become of his
dreams." Hobart and McIlvaine have guarded

different sides of the citadel of the church, but Muhlenberg has prevailed above all; so that he has come to be recognized as after all the truest leader of the Episcopal Church in America.

Dr. Muhlenberg was a real though an unconscious leader of religious thought. He was the herald of an age which came later; as the solitary German Uhlan first at Sedan told of the tread of the helmeted legions which were to come after, before whose compact strength the hollow empire of France must inevitably tumble down. He foresaw and made ready the way for those great movements which came afterwards in which the church of to-day rejoices, rather than directly marshaled in a conscious manner these nascent forces. But all true prophets are inspirers; and all true inspiration is leadership, though it may be unconscious leadership.

There was that in Dr. Muhlenberg's career which furnishes us with a striking illustration of the positive power of certain forms of negative influence. This seems at first sight to be a paradox, yet paradoxes very frequently contain the truth which inheres in the antitheses of the statement, in the same way in which the two abutments or piers of a bridge seem to imply the connecting span or arch. Too far east be-

comes the west again; and on this same line
of reasoning negative influence becomes after
a while a positive gain of power. When we
come to analyze its essential elements, we find
that influence is made up of reserve conviction
and manifested power. Both of these elements
were found in Dr. Muhlenberg's character. He
was not a bishop, nor a theologian, nor an intellectual leader in any way. He did not frequent clubs or clerical coteries; he did not write
brilliant papers for church congresses or mag-
azines; he was not in any sense an ecclesiastical
politician. He had undoubted tact, and this
magnetic and mysterious factor of success told
most unmistakably in the achievements of his
remarkable career. But it was never conscious
or officious tact, — that dreadful thing which
gives to the ward politician his command over
the primary caucus. Dr. Muhlenberg was not a
member of the standing committee of the diocese, nor a frequent delegate to the general convention; he was not a frequenter of clerical
gatherings, or church book-stores, or Episcopal
rooms, and was never a potent factor in any of
the meetings of the diocesan convention.

That which attracts so many of the younger
clergy, the ambition for place and the zeal for
ecclesiastical preferment (dreadful, pagan, un-
christlike word!), was entirely unknown to him.

In all this miserable arena of clerical ambition, where the Devil puts his cloven foot within the kingdom of God on the earth, and helps to pull the rope of those who are tugging at the wheels of the church, as if it were the car of Juggernaut, he was an entire stranger.

The type of churchmanship of which he was the creator was, as we have seen in a former chapter, something ideal, and spiritually commanding. It was not of the earth, earthy; it was that conception of church life which shows the presence of the Lord from heaven in the realm of the Prince of the power of the air.

The spirit of the age, the mere *Zeitgeist* conception of life, which so frequently invades with its withering touch the manifold works of the church of Christ in the world, never sullied the purity of his motives, or lamed the work of his hands. He realized the power there always is in truth; the power there is in the unworldly life; and he trusted to the sure verdict of the coming age to interpret that which he discovered his own generation was powerless to grasp. And it was this reserve of conviction, and this lavish absence of mere political skillfulness to handle the unready forces of his ecclesiastical day, which has given him his latent power, and has made him appear in the truest sense as one of the creators of our present American religious life. He did not spend his life in the mere details of ecclesiastical activity, but in living for that ideal, that heavenly vision, which had grasped his entire nature.

As these lines are penned, the writer is reminded of the words of the Russian leader and reformer, Count Leo Tolstoi, spoken in an interview recently held with him at his far-off home in Russia, — words which somehow seem to abide with a sense of their unmistakable power. "I will not organize," he said ; "it is enough if I can live according to my plan: it is the life which tells. Christ did not organize, he lived." And in like manner the negative influence of Dr. Muhlenberg shines at the last, by the side of his speaking life, as, after all, a gain of positive power.

It is Hegel who says that truth consists in holding opposite extremes, not in keeping safely to the boasted *via media* of the dusty turnpike road of commonplace conventionalities.

Dr. Muhlenberg is an illustration of this truth. He was a Catholic and he was a Protestant ; he was a Sacramentarian, and yet a believer in free prayer and evangelical preaching. He had that in his composition which was like Luther, and yet his sensitive conservatism made him sometimes take a position reminding one of Döllinger. He did not walk with the philosophers and theologians in Solomon's porch alone. He followed the Master down into the world's stony pavement, where truth has so often stood alone with Jesus before the judgment-seat of Cæsar's representative. He was not an official; he was a spirit, touching men in the wants of daily life; and he is living over again in a wonderful influence to-day, because he was distinctly one of that order of prophets which have been since the world began.

Moreover, he translated into our swift and practical American life the hidden riches of his German mind, stored as it was with that priceless treasure, — the magnetic wealth of mysticism. We have one such living voice among us yet, who, from his commanding tribune in New England's capital, reminds us of Savonarola in his best days of power and influence in the Medicean court of Florence.

Another gifted nature, touching the hearts of friends and followers with this same mystic fervor, has shown us the power of leadership on another line of thought, — and the church has been the richer and the better for the life and the faith of James De Koven.

Muhlenberg would have rejoiced alike in the pulpit of Boston and the school at Racine. For truth to his mind was ever found in the collocation of the antitheses of life, — the bringing together of the extremes of truth.

There was in his mind that picturesque element which has given such interest to the writings of Jacob Boehme, Herder, and Lessing, and has produced the wonderful musical creations from the imagination of Richard Wagner.

Muhlenberg was a greater prophet than Maurice on the practical side of life. He avoided dangerous by-currents and eddies; he kept well abreast of the wants of the age, and never loitered in the dark and morbid den of monastic or conventional sanctity. "I am evangelical," he used to say, "but not an evangelical with a capital letter E." In this way he never lost his clue, as so many reformers have done, from Savonarola to Lacordaire. Men who set out to reform the world most frequently speculate in thought and dabble in theories until they lose their bearings and go to pieces on the rocks, — because the unexpected has happened, and because, as with the Anti-Poverty Society of the present day, there have been too many warring theories of the way in which the ship should be sailed.

Then the nature which was once helpful and self-reliant becomes, as was the case with the gifted but unfortunate Edward Irving, like a spring that is dry where the great black insects burrow; or like a bell that is cracked and has no mellow sound reverberating from it; or like a

light that is burnt out and leaves only the charred
remembrance of bygone illuminations, and an
odor which tells of the oil of other days. Dr.
Muhlenberg always moved forward in a well-
defined course, and anchored definitely on his
own ground; he never drifted, and therefore he
never lost his bearings. After the defeat of the
Memorial Movement, he was content to rest on
the spot where apparent failure was the result of
his labors, and the generation which has come
after him has moved forward on parallel lines
of approach towards the goal of his consecrated
ambition!

Dr. Muhlenberg never substituted culture in
the place of spiritual force, as has been the fatal
mistake of the followers of Channing. Life is
too full of deep and awful meaning to be rightly
solved by any light and easy view of man's relationship to God, to the future, and to his fellow-
men. The Cavalier of old took life as a jest,
as he filled his glass to the memory of King
Charles; the Puritan took life as a tragedy, but
it was the Puritan, after all, who gave us the
age of Cromwell in England, and laid the foundations of that American commonwealth which
has recently been so profoundly analyzed by
the distinguished English author, who has pictured for us, in his other great work, the causes
of the rise of the Holy Roman Empire. Muh-

lenberg felt the presence of those moral forces
which had gone before him, and perceived that
if we would be the children of those who were
most truly our fathers, and would bring about
similar spiritual results in our life, we must
sow the vital seeds of our fathers' faith. He
felt that a theology which denies or belittles
the moral problems of existence belittles the nature of those who adopt it. He realized that
men may call their culture breadth, but that
there is a fatal narrowness in breadth when it ig-
nores or reduces to any subordinate position the
strong cravings of the spiritual life. He constantly maintained that this cry of humanity is
in every age the sign of God's essential nearness
to man, and that no system of philosophy, culture, metaphysics, or code of ethics can ever
meet and satisfy human nature's thirst for nothing less than the eternally living God. We
shall do well to ponder this trait in his character. A very liberal and eclectic spirit is abroad
to-day, and we delight in it, and we do well
thus to honor it. But with this ease of life,
and this luxury of environment, there comes a
lack of moral perception and of spiritual inward-
ness.

The cry to-day is for culture, not for character; for gifts and graces and accomplishments,
not for depth, trueness, and robustness A true,

unselfish man or woman shines in the crowds
of our great cities with a sort of solar light or
moral halo on the face. Great personalities
are becoming rare, — for it is only spiritual and
moral force which can create a great personality.
Culture alone is powerless in the sphere of creation. One never thought of the culture of Dr.
Muhlenburg; it was a side-chapel in the temple
of his being. But the central high altar towards
which all the lines of approach in his nature
turned was always spiritual force, — a dominat-
ing, creative, moral faculty.

Recklessness of belief, or the bowing of the
head at last to the decrees of destiny, is another
element in the common experience of most of
us which this favored worker for God seemed
wholly to avoid. He was never the slave of the
decree of fate. To most of history's conspicuous
workers, there are times in life when the philosophy of Omar Khayyám, the poet philosopher
of Persia, has a strange and mysterious fascina-
tion. The world's great men have been fatalists,
by a heathen or a Christian interpretation of
this doctrine, — by the philosophy of the Greek
dramatists, or by the inexorable logic of John
Calvin. There comes to most workers in the
world a time when they feel that the only solution of life is found in fatalism. St. Paul, Augustine, Calvin, Luther, Napoleon, Livingstone,

Lincoln, Gordon, the present Czar of Russia, and other men of destiny, have strangely realized this fact.

The reflex influence of many subtle forces tells most unmistakably in the life of every thinker and worker to-day. With the tables of political economy suggesting, with the broadest possible hint, that man is a drug and life is a wild fury signifying nothing, it becomes at times an extremely difficult task to maintain a steady habit of religious conviction in the presence of these dark denials of the faith.

Dr. Muhlenberg frequently felt that necessary reaction from the ideal and creative habit of mind, whose shadow in life is that strange and mysterious depression which was realized by our Lord upon the cross when he cried out, amid the gathering clouds of the mount of crucifixion, " Eloi, Eloi, lama sabachthani ! "

But depression is quite a different thing from mental recklessness and the bowing of the head to fate. It may be that depression in a certain sense is the necessary birth-pang of open and manifested work. Muhlenberg felt this cloud at times most keenly, and could have penned himself Matthew Arnold's words with reference to this mysterious and yet universal experience : —

" We cannot kindle when we will
   The fire which in the heart resides :
   The spirit bloweth and is still,
   In mystery our soul abides.
   But tasks in hours of insight willed
   Can be through hours of gloom fulfilled.

" With aching hands and bleeding feet,
   We dig and heap, lay stone on stone ;
   We leave the burden and the heat
   Of the long day, and wish 't were done.
   Not till the hours of light return
   All we have built do we discern."

Another striking element in his composition,
the very opposite of this quality of which we
have been speaking, was his conscious sense of
mental equipoise. The theoretical and the practical were most evenly balanced in his nature, and
he knew, as we have already seen, the unspeakable value of a well - trained mind. The faculty of coördination was, with him, developed to
a striking degree. He had the Napoleon mind
which always achieves successes on the field of
its exercise. He made his movements march :
they were not alone paper plans, spun out of
theory among the spider-webs of clerical club-
life. And he was preëminently a worker ; he
was not that mere talkative elderly gentleman
which many of the parochial stories in vogue
would lead us to imagine.

In the enervating environment of personal

fondness for our ministering heroes, we are in danger of forgetting the fundamental claim of manhood contained in Simon Peter's strong rebuke to Cornelius when he picked the man up who would have tumbled down before him, and, setting him upon his feet, exclaimed, "Stand up! I myself also am a man." The time has come for us to recognize the fact that Dr. Muhlenberg stands before the church on the basis of his own nobly achieved manhood. The day for the encircling nimbus of legendary dreamland is past and gone.

To combine strength with sweetness always implies the presence of a strong coördinating faculty. And Dr. Muhlenberg was strong as well as sweet, and here was the nerve-centre of his moral power. It happens to most of us in life that sooner or later one portion of our nature becomes definitely and distinctly arrayed against some other portion of our complex being. Knowledge stands upon one side; work stands on the other. Culture is arrayed against the plodding life of routine; attainments stand at one extreme, common sense stands at the other. Brilliancy of mind leads off in the race of life with a sparkling dash which seems to have in it the snap of victory; hard-headed endurance, and those qualities which seem born of the meaner or more plebeian portion of our nature, come up to the victor's stand at the end, and bear away the prize. In the great procession of life, the dreamers go before, and the drudges follow after, and the world has need for both of these classes. But somehow neither of them satisfies the age which brings them forth. If the dreamers only knew when to stop, if the drudges only knew when to go on, how much more satisfactory it would be !

But this man was both dreamer and drudge in one ; and his strong personality acquired its strength because of its successful coördination of these opposite extremes of character.

It is well for us to notice this trait of mental balance in his nature. The first thing that every true and wholesome worker must remember, as he leaves the door of the porch and the academy, is that his boasted culture is worse than useless unless it can be coördinated into the life of duty ; and that there are times when culture must be utterly forgotten and thrown aside whenever it stands as a block in the way of the transmission of knowledge through character into life. Dr. Muhlenberg might well have taken as his motto for his thoroughly coördinated life that defini-tion of duty which Mr. Gladstone has given in his reply to Cardinal Newman: " Duty," he wrote, " is a power which rises with us in the morning, and goes to rest with us at night. It is the shadow which cleaves to us, go where we will, and which never leaves us until we leave the light of life."

Dr. Muhlenberg possessed in a most marked degree the dual temperament of the poetic nature. He had a distinct and definite temperament of thought, and an equally marked temperament of feeling. He reasoned from the basis of the mind; he felt from the basis of the soul. In this way the element of caution was eliminated from his ceaseless activities; while at the same time the sensitiveness of his refined nature made him appear, to those who did not know him, at times shy and reserved. He was radical in thought and conservative in feeling, so that he was blamed alike at times by both schools of thought in the church, and in his day was understood by neither. The Evangelicals, as we have seen, called him a Sacramentarian; and Bishop Horatio Potter feared that he was leaning towards the Cummins movement, by his keen desire to move onward towards Christian unity, by the way of the Eucharistic service, with his brethren of the Evangelical Alliance, at the time when the Dean of Canterbury visited America. A lady who knew him well once expressed her sense of surprise at his dual nature by saying: "Dr. Muhlenberg, it is all right when I hear you preach, but it is all wrong when I see you in the chancel;" to which he wittily replied, "Quite right, madam; you know faith cometh by hearing." There is a story told of Bishop Fraser, of Manchester, that upon one occasion, at a certain congress in England, after his efforts to provide for the children of actors and actresses, in the movement then inaugurated towards the elevation of the stage, he was received upon the platform, when he rose to speak, with both cheers and hisses. Waiting until silence had been restored, he began as follows: "I thank my friends for this honest reception; some of you approve of that which I have recently done, and some of you, I perceive, disapprove of my action. That is right, for it is honest, and we Englishmen always appreciate honesty of expression. But, my friends," he continued, "unfortunately I am one of that class of men who not only have the courage of their convictions, but, thank God, have the courage also of their impulses." We are told not another expression of dissent was heard while the fearless bishop addressed the meeting, made up now entirely of friends.

And this trait of character was equally marked in Muhlenberg. He had not only the courage of his convictions, but he had also the courage of his impulses; and because of this twofold hold upon the future, he lives in his influence so powerfully to-day.

Another element of power in the character of
Muhlenberg was his free exercise of the moral
veto. He felt the mission of the veto power in
the realm of the spiritual world, and he was not
afraid to exercise it. Dr. Johnson once said
that, to be an interesting and a strong nature,
one must learn somewhere in life to become a
good hater, since there was so much in this world
that a good man ought to hate. Dr. Muhlenberg was at times a good hater, and was not
afraid to use the moral veto in rejecting much
that was weak, cowardly, superficial, and narrow
in the councils and actions of that church whose
boundless capacity he perceived with a prophet's
eye, but whose dangerous tendency to run into
the slough of the *via media* he constantly
condemned. This moral veto power in his nature he frequently exercised in his condemnation of those special ecclesiastical abominations
which, like whining dogs outside the church's
councils, were continually begging for admission
into the canonical and rubrical precincts of that
Mecca of all obstructionists, that ever-definite,
yet ever-illusive, far-off, millennial panacea for all
ills, the General Convention. But the moral and
spiritual barriers in Dr. Muhlenberg's nature
never gave way before the dull and solid on-
slaught of ecclesiastical superficialness, stupidity,
and Bourbonism of the apparently hopeless kind.

In the dark and heavy moments of defeat, disaster, and confusion of mind, the sure light of God's Spirit shone across the field of his vision like a light-house throwing its converging beams across the sea-meadow, when the fog from the ocean makes all things else seem misty and out of all perspective. Despite all show of failure, he still held resolutely on. The essential strength of his nature never gave way before the persistent attacks of superficial thought and life; and the definite light of faith in a conquering ideal always gave him ultimate peace and repose and calmness of mind. In his Memorial Movement, in seeking to unite the scattered branches of the church against the forces of evil in the world, he condemned the church's formalism and lack of divine compassion in preferring canonical exactness to evangelical obedience and practical American common sense. He condemned the perfunctory habit of mind in the church which maintained a resolute phalanx of opposition towards anything fresh and vital and new. And this judgment, which he fearlessly passed upon the temporizing policy of the church, has not been in vain. It has been his mission confessedly in life and conspicuously in death to lead the Episcopal Church, as with the divining rod of Moses, out of her traditional land of Egypt and house of bondage, so that the magnetic effect of his life has touched the lives of those who have come after him with brain-wave and with soul-wave, as the moon in the heavens commands at times the fretting and uncertain tides. Muhlenberg's life and force of character came into contact with an ecclesiastical system which was barely emerging from its period of colonial littleness, and he condemned, not the system, but the spirit which would not let it become developed, and his condemnation was the opening of its doors to liberty and life and power. His personality wrestled with an ecclesiastical mechanism which was strangely metallic, and he has been the inspired voice of God to fill that system with a life-giving, energizing spirit. Dr. Muhlenberg held a simple and definite creed, which insured for him, not the pleasures of speculation, but the delights of obedience. For there are certain things in life which, to all who would keep the faculty of leadership, must not become open questions again. "Men cannot waste their entire career in reviewing again and again the deepest principles by which their life is moulded, and they should cleave to those moral and spiritual assumptions with something like the obstinate fidelity with which a son cleaves to his parents, or a husband to his wife." [1] Dr. Muhlenberg never let the

[1] *London Spectator.*

ship of his faith lie-to in days of storm, to open
the hatches and inspect the cargo which has been
stowed away in the past. There were certain
things which to him were sealed for the re-
mainder of the voyage of life, — the fundamental
beliefs in God, in the future, and in the developing capacity of the human soul. It is in this
way that a strong life, such as the subject of the
present biography, tells upon those who come
within its range. We are all, at times in life,
like children in a forest who have lost the beaten
way, and are out of reach of the call of the
loving nurse, while the sun is sinking in the
west and the growing darkness of the night is
rapidly coming on. We are entangled by the
thickets in the complexity of life, and but for
the record of such strong characters as these we
would hopelessly lose our way. It is this which
makes true biography such helpful and inspiring reading. The Divine Warner of all souls
speaks to us most unmistakably by his revelation of truth and duty in the life and character
of his chosen and anointed ones.

In this way God becomes incarnate again and
again in every helpful spiritual life. For ourselves, we trust somehow that we shall each be
a success in life ; but the sound of our many
failures follows us like the clattering horsehoofs
of the steeds which are pressing after the win-

ner, — which may even yet snatch from the judge's stand the prize which we were sure was ours. And in the light of our own weakness and manifold mistakes, it is a divinely comforting fact to have an after-glow of influence illumine our path from God's saints who in every age have achieved success where we see only failure. Thus, in the light and influence of God's latest saints, we realize once more the meaning of that far-off record given with so much confidence to the Hebrew Christians of the first century : —

" And what shall I more say ? for the time will fail me if I tell of Gideon, Barak, Samson, Jephtha ; of David, and Samuel, and the prophets : who through faith subdued kingdoms, wrought righteousness, obtained promises, stopped the mouths of lions, quenched the power of fire, escaped the edge of the sword, from weakness were made strong, waxed mighty in war, turned to flight armies of aliens. Women received their dead by a resurrection : and others were tortured, not accepting their deliverance ; that they might obtain a better resurrection : and others had trial of mockings and scourgings ; yea, moreover of bonds and imprisonment : they were stoned, they were sawn asunder, they were tempted, they were slain with the sword : they went about in sheepskins, in goatskins ; being destitute, afflicted, evil-entreated (of whom the world was not worthy), wandering in deserts and mountains and caves, and the holes of the earth. And these all, having had witness borne to them through their faith, received not the promise, God having provided some better thing concerning us, that apart from us they should not be made perfect." [1]

Dr. Muhlenberg was patient in the happening of the unexpected in his life. He calmly waited, after the failure of the Memorial Movement, for the day when the church would see that he was right, — another Athanasius *contra mundum* ; and when the congress of churches thirty years later fulfilled his original ideal, all who were familiar with the story of Dr. Muhlenberg's life knew that this creation was his far-off dream at last realized. It is always soul which tells on soul. It is not position, office, function, pomp, or power. There always have been prophets in the church of the living God, and this man was one of these. He was a philanthropist and a poet, but he was also more than this : he was a prophet with a level head and a well-trained mind. When he lived and was a worker, men said he was a dreamer. Now that he is dead we forget his dreams, as we see only the record of his realized works — in brick and stone and mortar — in college and hospital, home, church, and cathedral, and in a definite movement of American Christianity towards a national and historic church of the English-speaking race in the freedom of the American commonwealth,

[1] Hebrews xi. 32–40, Revised Version.

where all old things are being tried again under newer, freer, and better conditions whereby to insure their ultimate success. And now the story of this life is told.

A preface to a book ought to be like the overture in music. The principal arias of the after-work ought therein to be unmistakably indicated.

Thus, as these closing lines are penned, let us go back in thought to what was said at the beginning of the life of this representative character in the Episcopal Church. He had the sense of vision, which is the function of the prophet; he had the gift of discerning of spirits, which is the test of all true apostleship; and he possessed the faculty to make his movements move, which is the witnessing sign of the creative genius. Let us leave him, then, side by side with the other leaders of American religious thought, — with Channing and Edwards and Bushnell and Wilbur Fisk and Hodge and Washburn and Alexander Campbell and Mulford, — while the after-glow of his influence seems like the reflected glory of the mount of the Master's Transfiguration. He has done his work; his influence is a living power to-day, and —

"No work begun shall ever pause for death."

APPENDIX A.

THE following is the version of 1876 of the hymn, "I would not live alway:" —

"I would not live alway — I ask not to stay,
For nought but to lengthen the term of the way;
Nay, fondly I've hoped, when my work-days were done,
Then, soon and undim'd, would go down my life's sun.

"But, if other my lot, and I'm destined to wait
Thro' suffering and weakness in useless estate,
Till I gain my release, gracious Lord keep me still,
Unmurmuring, resigned to thy Fatherly will.

"Yea, thus let it be, so that thereby I grow
More meet for his presence to whom I would go,
More patient, more loving, more quiet within,
Throughly washed in the Fountain that cleanseth from sin.

"So the days of my tarrying on to their end,
Bringing forth what they may, all in praise I would spend:
Then, no cloud on my faith, when called for I'd leave,
Calm in prayer, 'Lord Jesus, my spirit receive.'

"But inside the veil, — How, how is it there?
Dare we ask for some sight, or some sound to declare,
What the blessed are doing — afar or anear?
Oh! but for a whisper, the darkness to cheer!

"Yet, why aught of darkness? Light, light enough this,
The Paradise life, — it can be only bliss;
And whatever its kind, or where'er its realm lies,
The Saviour its glory, the Sun of its skies."

APPENDIX B.

In view of the general interest in the subject of Christian Unity, which has recently occupied the minds of the American churches of all names, the following declaration of the House of Bishops is added as an emphatic underscoring of the position taken by Dr. Muhlenberg upon this subject, and as the historic realization of his original proposition made thirty years ago in the "Memorial Movement," of which he was the author, as well as to show that Dr. Muhlenberg's original proposition is implied in this official manifesto : —

Action of the House of Bishops at the General Convention at Chicago, October, 1886.

We do hereby solemnly declare to all whom it may concern, and especially to our fellow-Christians of the different communions in this land, who in their several spheres have contended for the religion of Christ, —

1. Our earnest desire that the Saviour's prayer, "that we may all be one," may, in its deepest and truest sense, be speedily fulfilled.

2. That we believe that all who have been duly baptized with water, in the name of the Father, and of the Son, and of the Holy Ghost, are members of the Holy Catholic Church.

3. That in all things of human ordering or human choice, relating to modes of worship and discipline, or to traditional customs, this church is ready, in the

spirit of love and humility, to forego all preferences of her own.

4. That this church does not seek to absorb other communions, but rather, coöperating with them on the basis of a common faith and order, to discontinue schism, to heal the wounds of the body of Christ, and to promote the charity which is the chief of Christian graces, and the visible manifestation of Christ to the world.

But, furthermore, we do hereby affirm that the Christian unity, now so earnestly desired by the memorialists, can be restored only by the return of all Christian communions to the principles of unity exemplified by the undivided Catholic Church, during the first ages of its existence ; which principles we believe to be the substantial deposit of Christian faith and order committed by Christ and the apostles to the church unto the end of the world, and therefore incapable of compromise or surrender by those who have been ordained to be its stewards and trustees for the common and equal benefit of all men. As inherent parts of this sacred deposit, and therefore as essential to the restoration of unity among the divided branches of Christendom, we account the following, to wit : —

1. The Holy Scriptures of the Old and New Testament as the revealed word of God.

2. The Nicene Creed as the sufficient statement of the Christian faith.

3. The two sacraments — Baptism, and the Supper of the Lord — ministered with unfailing use of Christ's

words of institution, and of the elements ordained by Him.

4. The local episcopate, locally adapted in the methods of its administration to the varying needs of the nations and people called of God into the unity of his church.

Furthermore, deeply grieved by the sad divisions which afflict the Christian church in our own land, we hereby declare our desire and readiness, so soon as there shall be any authorized response to this declaration, to enter into brotherly conference with all or any Christian bodies seeking the restoration of the organic unity of the church, with a view to the earnest study of the conditions under which so priceless a blessing might happily be brought to pass.

The following suggestion as to a practical basis of Christian union, from a Presbyterian, appeared in " The Churchman " of October 26, 1889 : —

" *To the Editor of The Churchman :*

" While the writer would probably be regarded as standing in the opposite wing of the Presbyterian body to Professor Briggs, he agrees entirely with him in holding as satisfactory the basis of Christian union proposed by the House of Bishops of the American Episcopal Church and revised by the Lambeth Conference. The first three terms, the Scriptures, the Creeds, and the Sacraments, could hardly cause serious discussion among Protestants. All accept them, not, of course, as expressing all that any one perhaps believes on those points, but all that is essential to Christian faith. We are unable to see why there should be any more difficulty with the 'historic episcopate.' We may differ in accounting for it, as Episcopalians themselves differ, but the historic episcopate itself is an admitted fact. Calvin admitted it. The best historic scholarship of our age admits it. The House of Bishops made their deliverance intelligently and honestly. They do not ask us, as we understand them, to accept any particular theory of the episcopate. They ask us to accept the fact, and there is the fact, whether we accept it or not. We are unable to see a simpler basis of union than this.

"Whether any organic union of denominations is likely to be effected soon on this basis may be a question. But another question will certainly emerge. It is that of individual action. In the strong longing for Christian unity there will be those, there are those, who will turn to the action of the bishops to study its bearing on their personal duty. Will the terms laid down be the terms for individuals as well as for churches? Will the full and cordial acceptance of that basis be sufficient for the reception of ministers of other bodies to the Episcopal ministry? We do not raise the question of reimposition of hands. We are not strenuous about that. In the New Testament, ministers had hands laid upon them more than once. But as the law now stands in the Episcopal Church, there is this practical difficulty. The most devoted minister of another denomination, with whatever years of service behind him, must give proof of his character through at least a year of waiting before he can serve in the Episcopal Church. The general wisdom of this rule, for the circumstances in which it was intended to apply, is unquestioned. But will it be wise to insist on it in the changing conditions that may lie before the church? Would it be necessary to require Dr. Storrs of Brooklyn, or Dr. William M. Taylor of New York, to give a year's silent proof of their fitness for service in the Episcopal Church? Should not the bishops have discretion in such cases? Must they not have it to meet the spirit and the letter of the action of the House of Bishops and the Lambeth Conference? Would not the settlement of this question be eminently worthy the present convention?   A Presbyterian."

APPENDIX C.

THE following anecdotes of Dr. Muhlenberg at St. Luke's Hospital, never before written down, have been kindly sent in by Mrs. E. W. C. Hall, from her own personal experience. A lady who was for many years a regular visitor to the public institutions of New York city said of Dr. Muhlenberg, that his sympathy and gentleness of manner were so spontaneous and unvarying, that she never approached him in St. Luke's Hospital without a perfect assurance that he would receive her kindly, and if possible grant her request.

In those days, the nurses provided for the sick on Blackwell's Island were prisoners from the work-house, and were usually in a semi-intoxicated con-dition, as they did not hesitate to appropriate to themselves the whiskey ordered for the patients. This led to cruelties almost too dreadful to mention. That and other grievances with which Dr. Muhlen-berg was familiar touched his heart with deep sor-row, and so, when accommodations at St. Luke's were insufficient for the demand, he would sometimes turn from those who had a pastor or friends to look after them, and receive in their stead sufferers who were at the mercy of attendants, brutal in their nature and in their treatment of the helpless and dying.

In one of the wards of Charity Hospital lay a Christian man, whose painful surroundings were so at variance with his beautiful character, it seemed to the visitor a high duty to find for him a more con-genial resting-place, where he could spend the few remaining days of his life in the comforts of those blessed privileges provided by our mother the church. When his story was related to the warm-hearted pas-tor of St. Luke's, he at once consented to receive the sufferer, with the understanding that his end was in all probability near at hand. The rules of the insti-tution did not permit a consumptive to enter, when there was a prospect of his having a long and hope-less illness, thereby shutting out those who might be soon benefited, and in turn give place to others.

When the sick man was taken to St. Luke's, Dr. Muhlenberg was asked if he might remain there as long as he lived. The pastor before replying called in the examining physician, who said he could not possibly linger more than two months. So the pastor, with a happy cheerfulness of manner, assured the visitor who took the patient there that he might "remain to the end of his days." It was most touching to witness Dr. Muhlenberg's devotion to that poor man, who received special attention from doctors and nurses, and who was allowed all the religious privileges so lovingly provided in the hospital. When the invalid was able to sit up, the holy communion was celebrated at his bedside, the thoughtful pastor sending an invitation to his lady friend to be present.

Amid such genial surroundings, the consumptive grew better, and lived two years before being called to his rest. Meanwhile he became a centre of happy influence to those around him. When his friend the visitor was herself ill, he was able to go quite a distance to her residence to express his interest, and to tell of his gratitude for such a haven of rest. Dr. Muhlenberg, on meeting this lady in the hospital, often referred, with a twinkle in his eye, to one patient he had who would "never die."

Dr. Muhlenberg once received from Charity Hospital a very pleasing young man belonging to the better class of patients, prepared him for baptism and confirmation, again sending for the lady visitor to be present at his first reception of the holy communion. Subsequently he sent this patient out into the world, a well man physically, and a happy, earnest child of the church.

A student in the General Theological Seminary, young and delicate, when taken seriously ill, far from home and kindred, was welcomed to the peaceful shelter of St. Luke's, watched over and cheered by the pastor in his own inimitable way, and then by him committed, as he was about to leave this world, to the care of One who would be with him and comfort him through the valley of the shadow of death to his joyful home beyond.

A man in middle life, vigorous and full of zeal, who had nearly completed his theological course, was seized with typhoid fever, brought on largely by overwork and special efforts in visiting prisoners in the penitentiary. He was taken to St. Luke's, where his lady friend, with whom he usually visited the institutions, called to see him. He was suffering from intense thirst, and longing for something to cool his parched lips. As Dr. Muhlenberg stood by, and listened to his pathetic pleadings, he at once sought and consulted the physician, and as a result, recognizing probably that the case seemed quite hopeless, it was decided to grant his request. The pastor went himself and quickly returned with a bowl of cracked ice, which he gave to the sufferer with his own hands as tenderly as a father would minister to his son.

Still another student from the same seminary, now a well-known priest in the church, expressed so much gratitude, after his recovery at St. Luke's, that a friend, in preparing a little memorial wreath for him to take to his distant parish in the West, ventured to ask Dr. Muhlenberg's permission to pluck for the wreath one small flower from the beautiful grounds of the hospital, around which clustered such precious recollections. The doctor gave his consent, and when the lady, who had spent one hour in visiting certain patients in the upper wards, came down the steps, great was her surprise to find the kind-hearted pastor still waiting and watching for her, with a large cluster of the choicest blossoms, which he gathered with his own hands, to send to the appreciative clergyman with his " brotherly love."

On the anniversary of Washington's birthday, the visitor called to ask permission for a Welshman, who was dangerously ill, to enter the hospital. The chimes of St. Thomas's Church, on the next block, were ringing in honor of the day ; and though the pastor was engaged with friends who were to dine with him, he at once responded to the call, but said there was " no vacancy." However, on learning the urgency of the case, and how worthy of special kindness was the Christian man who had given the last of his strength in a church choir where he had long rendered acceptable service, he said, with sympathy in his voice, " Well, he can come — I will *make* room for him." That was the last patient dear Dr. Muhlenberg ever received into St. Luke's Hospital, for a few hours later the same day he was stricken with the illness from which he never recovered. His appearance on that occasion, with a purple cap on his head, from beneath which his long silvery locks hung down over a becoming purple gown that reached to his feet, was very striking, and the visitor has often wished that his picture could have been taken at the moment when, in the kindness of his tender heart, he said, while Christian love lighted up his features, " Well, he can come — I will *make* room for him."

An intelligent young woman, who spent several of her early years in St. Luke's, recalls one scene which is vividly impressed on her memory. The children all loved Dr. Muhlenberg dearly, and when he entered the children's ward in the hospital they ran to him, caught hold of his hands and arms, clung to the skirts of his coat, and completely surrounded him, while he marched with them through the ward, singing in loud and spirited tones, while the children's voices blended in the strain, " Praise God from whom all blessings flow," and on to the end of the Doxology. It must have been, as she describes it, a touching and beautiful sight, and, as she proves it to have been, one always to be remembered.

INDEX.

———◆———

American Religious Leaders.

A Series of Biographies of Men who have had great
influence on Religious Thought and
Life in the United States.

JONATHAN EDWARDS. By Professor A. V. G.
Allen, author of "The Continuity of Christian Thought."

WILBUR FISK. By Professor George Prentice, of
Wesleyan University.

DR. MUHLENBERG. By Rev. William Wilberforce
Newton.

FRANCIS WAYLAND. By Professor J. O. Mur-
ray, of Princeton.

ARCHBISHOP JOHN HUGHES. By John G.
Shea, LL. D., author of "The Catholic Authors of America," etc.

CHARLES HODGE. By President Francis L. Pat-
ton, of Princeton.

THEODORE PARKER. By John Fiske, author of
"The Idea of God," "Outlines of Cosmic Philosophy," etc.

CHARLES G. FINNEY. By Professor G. Frederick
Wright.

This Series will include biographies of eminent men
who represent the theology and methods of the various religious denominations of America, yet the object of the Series does not contemplate emphasizing
personal character and history except as these are related to the development of religious thought or the
quickening of religious life. The Series when completed will not only depict in a clear and memorable
way several great figures in American religious history, but will indicate the leading characteristics of
that history, the progress and process of religious
philosophy in America, the various types of theology
which have shaped or been shaped by the various
churches, and the relation of these to the life and
thought of the Nation.

---

*Other volumes to be announced hereafter. Each volume, 16mo, gilt
top, $1.25.*

HOUGHTON, MIFFLIN & COMPANY,

4 PARK ST., BOSTON; 11 EAST 17TH ST., NEW YORK.

American Men of Letters.

Edited by Charles Dudley Warner.

WASHINGTON IRVING. By Charles Dudley Warner, author of "In the Levant," etc.

NOAH WEBSTER. By Horace E. Scudder, author of "Stories and Romances," "A History of the United States of America," etc.

HENRY D. THOREAU. By Frank B. Sanborn.

GEORGE RIPLEY. By Octavius Brooks Frothingham, author of "Transcendentalism in New England."

JAMES FENIMORE COOPER. By Thomas R. Lounsbury, Professor of English in the Scientific School of Yale College.

MARGARET FULLER OSSOLI. By Thomas Wentworth Higginson, author of "Malbone," "Oldport Days," etc.

RALPH WALDO EMERSON. By Oliver Wendell Holmes, author of "The Autocrat of the Breakfast-Table," etc.

EDGAR ALLAN POE. By George E. Woodberry, author of "A History of Wood Engraving."

NATHANIEL PARKER WILLIS. By Henry A. Beers, Professor of English Literature in Yale College.

BENJAMIN FRANKLIN. By John Bach McMaster, author of "History of the People of the United States."

In Preparation.

NATHANIEL HAWTHORNE. By James Russell Lowell, author of "My Study Windows," etc.

WILLIAM CULLEN BRYANT. By John Bigelow, author of "Molinos the Quietist," etc.

Other volumes to be announced hereafter. Each volume, with Portrait, 16mo, gilt top, $1.25 ; half morocco, $2.50.

HOUGHTON, MIFFLIN & COMPANY,

4 PARK ST., BOSTON ; 11 EAST 17TH ST , NEW YORK.

American Statesmen.

Edited by John T. Morse, Jr.
